Go, Get 'Em!

SNAPSHOT OF THE AUTHOR,
TAKEN "SOMEWHERE IN FRANCE"

Go, Get 'Em!

An American Aviator in the Lafayette
Flying Corps During the First World War

William A. Wellman

LEONAUR

Go, Get 'Em!
An American Aviator in the Lafayette Flying Corps During the First World War
by William A. Wellman

First published under the title
Go, Get 'Em

Leonaur is an imprint of Oakpast Ltd

Copyright in this form © 2012 Oakpast Ltd

ISBN: 978-0-85706-812-5 (hardcover)
ISBN: 978-0-85706-813-2 (softcover)

http://www.leonaur.com

Contents

To
My
Little Mother

Introduction

It was a drowsy, peaceful day in early May. War seemed remote, an evil unreality. Lured from my writing by the insistent call of Spring, I left my desk and strolled instinctively toward Boston's breathing space, the "Common" of historic memories, whose easterly mall, honoured in bearing the name of Lafayette, was now lined with a row of trim green and white cottages dedicated to the comfort of the boys who wear the khaki or the blue.

Before the little stage in front of one I saw gathered a thronging crowd that, from a distance, gave the impression of many drones clustered about the opening of a hive.

Such assemblages had become every-day sights and I moved toward it, impelled by a mild curiosity merely; but, when my eyes fell upon the figure which was leaning over the railing in an attitude of stirring appeal, my steps quickened.

The form was that of a stalwart young man clad in the horizon blue of the French army. The uniform stirred my pulses, but it was not that alone which now drew me, magnetlike.

It was rather that, even from my distance, I could recognize the bearing and familiar gestures of a youth whom I had known from his childhood and had seen grow up into young manhood from a lad after whom Mark Twain might well have patterned his "Tom Sawyer," or T. B. Aldrich *his* "bad boy."

I pressed my way through the eagerly listening crowd until I was close enough to the speaker to see the two-winged gold and silver insignia of the *Lafayette Flying Corps*, the bronze *Croix de Guerre* suspended from a ribbon upon which gleamed two palm leaves of victory, and, above it, the narrow strip of multi-coloured cloth which mutely told the story of a wound received in service.

Others were drinking in the lad's stories of battles waged in mid-air by the immortal Gunemeyer,[1] Frank Baylies, David Putnam and Tom Hitchcock—one of them dead, one soon to make the supreme sacrifice and one a hapless prisoner to the Hun;—but my thoughts would not behave, and rather kept racing back to those days, so short a while ago, when I had seen the boy dashing down the field on a quarterback run to win a hard fought game for Newton High; stopping a difficult grounder at short, and, with ease and precision, snapping the ball to first base ahead of an eager runner; or outflying the skating pack in a hockey rink; for, prior to going "over there "to take a notable part in the greatest game of all, he had been an athlete *par excellence.*

Spoken unconcernedly came the words, "My *Nieuport* flew a hundred and thirty miles an hour, unless the wind was with it, when. . ." and I shuddered involuntarily, for I remembered the first and only time that I had entrusted my precious life to a motorcycle, having climbed up behind the speaker upon his promise to go slowly, only to be whisked through the streets at a speed which seemed to me fully to equal that of the flying *Nieuport.*

"You folks think that you are getting a taste of war rations. You don't know what they are," the voice continued. "Why, when I landed in New York the waiter apologetically served me with what he called 'war bread.' I thought that it was *cake.*" The audience laughed, and his sally took me back to the days when, as a mere lad, he had starred in every local show, as comedian, dancer and singer.

The lad sold another thousand dollars' worth of War Saving Stamps, and ended his informal talk with the words, "I have sometimes been called 'a hero,' but I want to tell you men that I am nothing of the kind. The *real* heroes of this war are the boys in the trenches, who often stand for days in snow, or mud and water up to their knees; who eat what they can get, and when they can get it; and who never have their names in the paper unless they are wounded or killed. *They* are the heroes."

Followed by a prolonged burst of applause, he stepped down, and a husky sailor lad sprang into the vacated place and shouted, "I want to take issue with what Sergeant Wellman has just said. He has told you something of what those chaps of the Lafayette Flying Corps have been doing in the air, though mighty little about himself—it wasn't necessary, you read the papers;—but I want to say to him and to you,

---

1. *Guynemer: Chevalier of the Air* by Henry Bordeaux & Mary R. Parkman, (*Georges Guynemer, Knight of the Air* by Henry Bordeaux and *The Chevalier of Flight: Captain Guynemer* by Mary R. Parkman), also published by Leonaur.

that a fellow who has been through what he has, is one hundred *per cent.* a *man.*"

We thrill upon meeting an American hero of the great conflict; the thrill is increased if that hero is a townsman of ours; but, if he is also a close friend of long years' standing, it is the greatest of all, and, as I pushed my way forward to grasp the sinewy, bronzed hand of Billy Wellman, the American daredevil of *Escadrille* N. 87, Lafayette Flying Corps, I thought that none but a real live Yankee lad could have done all that he had done for France and the great Cause, and yet carry his honours so modestly. And my heart echoed the words, "one hundred *per cent.* a *MAN.*"

Eliot Harlow Robinson.

CHAPTER 1

Overseas

On the forenoon of Saturday, the twenty-ninth day of March, Nineteen hundred and Seventeen, I came dejectedly out from beneath the gilded dome of the Massachusetts State House on Beacon Hill, having just been rejected for admission to the Naval Aviation service of the United States.

On the forenoon of Friday, the twenty-ninth day of March, Nineteen hundred and *Eighteen* I was honourably discharged, because of injuries received in action, from the Lafayette Flying Corps of the historic Foreign Legion of France. I had, eight days previous, been shot down from a height of something over three miles above the lines in Lorraine, held by the Rainbow boys of General Pershing's original Expeditionary Force.

The twelve months' period which intervened between those two dates covers what I have reason to believe will be the most interesting and thrilling chapter in my *Book of Life* when it is finally closed. Yet, unlike many chapters of "hair breadth 'scapes and moving accidents," I would be only too glad to live it—or most of it—over again, and it is my sincerest hope that, before the present ghastly war is ended, I may at least have the chance of living out its sequel, in the uniform of my own country.

I write this in no spirit of bloodthirstiness or bravado. I have more reason than most for wanting to see the war end, and my hope that it may not, until I am able to get back into the fight among the clouds, is based upon the firm belief that an early peace would mean but one thing—*VICTORY FOR THE HUN!*

And "Peace without Victory," or *any* peace, short of a complete and crushing victory for America and her allies, would spell a world catastrophe.

13

This story of my year in the French service is not to be in any sense a treatise on what a Prussian victory would mean to civilization; but, before I have finished my narrative, I hope that I shall have shown you in some measure why I feel as I do.

That is my primary object in writing it; the secondary one is in order that those who chance to read it may have a fuller conception of what air fighting means and is, for it has already become a great factor in warfare, and will, I firmly believe, become the greatest factor in achieving the ultimate decision.

Finally, I hope that the story of my experiences and battles may—in some measure—"stiffen the sinews and summon up the blood" of the youth of America, so that all, who are able, will go and do likewise, and in fuller measure than has yet been possible in my case.

It is a fascinating game—this flying and fighting in the air—and it cannot but appeal to every red-blooded Yankee, for we are a nation of athletes, and I can truly say, having tried my hand at almost all branches of sport, that none other begins to compare with it.

Probably, indeed, it was the sporting instinct which first drew me into the great conflict, for I cannot lay claim to having had any heroic idea of yielding myself a sacrifice for the cause of humanity, although something approaching that spirit may have later been engendered in me, as it must be in every man who, at close range, sees the Barbarous Hun in his assault on everything that is pure, fair and worthwhile in the world.

Nor can I lay claim to any remarkable foresight in anticipating in March that America would soon be mixed up in the fight, and in trying to get into it in the branch of the service that most appealed to me.

At the time when my decision was made I was twenty years old, living in Cambridge, Massachusetts, and engaged in the wool business, and for some time I had looked forward to nothing more exciting in life than the everyday battle in that highly peaceful pursuit. Nevertheless, the germ of adventure was in my blood and, as I have hinted, every form of athletic exercise and conflict had always strongly appealed to me. I had engaged in almost every kind, too, while in the Newton High School—where I suppose I had the reputation of being a pretty bad boy—and I had fought, boxed, played football, baseball, hockey and every kind of a mad prank all my life.

Doubtless these all had a part in making me physically fit for what was coming, for although, when my major adventure began, I was but five feet nine and one-half inches tall and weighed only one hundred and forty pounds, I was as "hard as nails." Incidentally, while I was "over there" I increased my height one inch and my weight eighteen pounds.

Some little time before the date of my decision, the United States had established a training school for naval aviators at Squantum, only a few miles from Boston, on the old field which was once a place famous for the earliest aerial meets. The newspaper accounts of the work being carried on there, and the occasional sight of an airplane passing high over the city had stirred my imagination and my eagerness to fly, too, until it could not be repressed.

Without announcing my determination to anyone, I went to the State House and put in my application for enlistment in the air-branch of the service.

The officer in charge of the enlistments questioned me briefly about my life, and, when he asked me if I were a college graduate and I answered in the negative, he told me that there was no chance for me then, and added that the service was full and probably would be for some time.

Somehow this rejection, after I had set my mind upon getting into the big game in which I felt that America was soon to play an active part, fixed my determination to do *something*, and do it quick.

Several chums of mine had already enlisted in, and returned from, ambulance work at the front,[2] and during the next few days, while I was on the road on business, I thought the matter over seriously. One evening, in the week which followed, I was in Worcester; and while there suddenly made up my mind to join one of the American ambulance units, and go to France for the purpose of helping *French* and English lives, if I was not to be allowed to prepare myself to take German ones. A rector, living in my old home city of Newton, had told me about the Harjes-Norton Ambulance Corps of New York, and I made up my mind to get into that, if I could.

Acting impulsively on the idea I called Mr. Norton—its American sponsor—by long distance telephone, explained my desire to him, and asked if I might see him and be examined. His answer was a prompt, "Yes."

Still keeping my plans almost wholly to myself I obtained letters

---

2. *"Ambulance 464" Encore Des Blessés* by Julien H. Bryan, (the experiences of an American Volunteer with the French Army during the First World War), also published by Leonaur.

of recommendation from Professor Samuel Williston, of the Harvard Law School, a relative of mine, and the Reverend Edward Sullivan, of Grace (Episcopal) Church in Newton Centre, in whose choir I had formerly sung, and went at once to see Mr. Norton,—a splendid type of American who had, I was told, practically given up a big law practice to engage voluntarily in that glorious work.

He talked pleasantly with me for a few moments, asked me if I could drive an automobile and, upon being told that I could, accepted my services. I signed for the customary six months' period.

Upon my return home I told my family what I had done, and, although it was not difficult to see that the news came as a shock to my little mother, she merely smiled and told me that she was glad that I had taken the step.

The period of waiting for notice to leave for France was passed impatiently, for I have always wanted to do things in a hurry. Meanwhile America entered the war; but the die was cast as far as I was concerned—what the future might hold here was problematical, and I was only confirmed in my decision to get to the front at once.

Word came at last. I was to sail on the French liner, *Rochambeau*—most appropriately named, as it eventuated—on the twenty-second day of May.

Accompanied by my mother, I went to New York in time to receive my equipment, which included a well-filled duffle bag and everything but the uniform, and on the scheduled day I said my farewells and boarded the ship bound overseas.

The *Rochambeau*, although a second-class liner, was fast. She carried a good-sized, mixed passenger list, some of my fellow voyagers being French people returning home; but in the main they were Americans who were "going over" for purposes connected with the war—among them Miss Anne Morgan, whose work for the Red Cross has been so wonderful.

My small stateroom held four bunks, and two of my roommates and new acquaintances—who were also going to join units of the American Ambulance corps—warrant a word of mention.

One was a Mr. Brown of Minneapolis, whom, because of his size and rotundity, we called "Buster." Like most men of avoirdupois he was good-natured and jolly, and kept me laughing the whole trip. One of his favourite pranks was to climb into his upper berth long after the occupant of the one beneath it had gone to bed and to sleep, using the latter's face as a stepladder.

The other, with whom I became closely acquainted, was "Bill" Cody, from Chicago—a tall, splendidly proportioned young chap, who was as wild a Westerner as ever had been his world-famous uncle, "Buffalo Bill."

Another of the passengers with whom I early struck up a warm friendship was a man who had apparently been selected by Fate as her agent in changing the course of my life. This was Reginald Sinclair, of New York, familiarly known as "Duke," and he was a prince. Later he was to be my close companion in the flying school, and the biggest man there, for he stood over six feet-two, and was in build the type which is now winning for our "Sammies" the vigorous name of "Huskies." "Duke" was not an Adonis, nor was it his wealth that earned him a place well entrenched in our hearts, but it was because he was a good sport and so generous that he would any time have given the shirt off his back to help a friend. Perhaps the expression is not well chosen, for at Avord most of us were quite willing to get our shirts off, for reasons which you will read later.

He was going over expressly to enlist in the Lafayette Flying Corps, and, as we became acquainted, and he told me about his plans and the work of that organization, he planted the seeds of desire anew in my own mind. During the trip they grew rapidly, and, by the time I had reached France, I was crazy to change over, especially as my companions told me that it was done frequently, and that the Harjes-Norton Corps was only too glad to have its men do it.

There was also another man on board who was going for the same purpose as Sinclair; but I shall not mention his name—it is not a popular one among American aviators of the Lafayette Corps. It is enough to say that he failed to graduate from the first—or "ground"—class in the school at Avord; but, when he returned to America, he lectured extensively on aviation and "fighting in the air."

During the trip over I proved to my own satisfaction that I was a good sailor, for I was not sick, although the Atlantic was very rough. Aside from the tossing we got, the voyage was uneventful, and but two incidents on shipboard stand out in my memory as worthy of record.

One had to do with a slender little clergyman, and a fascinating little French actress who was returning to Paris after performing all winter with the French Players in New York. The passengers held a Red Cross benefit performance in the main saloon one evening, and her act was the last on the bill, the announcement being made that she would be auctioned off to the highest bidder, whose would be the

17

privilege of kissing her.

She was brought in, dressed to represent a flower, the clothes basket which contained her being the flower pot, and her singing and dancing act was a tremendous hit. Then the bidding began at a lively rate, and in the midst of it the little minister appeared in the doorway. He was just in time to hear the bid, "one-twenty-five," called out. The next was "two-fifty," and he stepped forward eagerly and bid "three." Moreover he stayed in the game until he had bought her for "five."

Like a good sport, although not without embarrassment, he advanced to kiss her, amid laughter, cheers and applause.

"First pay the five hundred *francs*," cried the auctioneer.

"Five *hundred francs*," gasped the minister. "Why, I . . . I thought it was *five*." It was a facer for him, but he came to the mark, although he had to borrow from all his friends in order to do it. I rather guess that the experience taught him a salutary lesson about mixing with Mammon.

The other incident occurred one morning when we were two days' distant from our destination. We had been sailing unconvoyed, and undisturbed by the new devils of the deep, although every precaution had been taken to guard against them, such as the closing and darkening of all portholes with steel covers and canvas, and the "dousing" of every "glim" on deck at night.

I was on deck, looking idly across the sailless sea and wondering if I should ever behold a submarine, when the ship suddenly veered almost at right angles to her former course, and the lookout cried out excitedly and pointed over the bow. There, bisecting our path, and only a few yards away, was a moving white line which beyond doubt marked the course of a deadly torpedo.

The U-boat from which it had been shot was not to be seen; but, for some hours, the *Rochambeau* zigzagged and twisted like the pursued in a game of hare and hounds, and on that, and the following, night we were forced to remain fully dressed on deck or in the main cabin.

Nothing happened, and there was little excitement manifested by the passengers; but it is safe to say that the feeling of imminent danger was in everybody's mind.

I passed the trip in playing cards and idling, for the most part; but I managed to turn a little time to profit by picking up some rudimentary French from two charming Parisian children and their pretty nursemaid, who were among those returning home.

18

Ten days after we left America the shores of southern France showed on the eastern horizon and brought to me the thrill that every argonaut must feel when the land which holds his particular golden fleece first appears before him. Our first stop was to be Bordeaux, and, as we entered the ever narrowing Garonne River and sailed close to the banks, I gained my first impression of the new old-world. It was a pleasing one.

In the distance the country rose in rolling hillocks, and near at hand on either side I could see the beautifully cultivated squared off fields and the odd little villages, over the cobbled streets of which bumped antiquated appearing buggies.

This sail upriver brought me also the first aspect of war, for we passed so close to a big fence-enclosed field with rough barracks on one side, and holding several hundred German prisoners, that the passengers shouted out invectives at them. They merely gazed stolidly back.

Presently we docked and were examined by the custom and army officials, but my own examination was cursory, for my passport explained my mission, and it took only a moment to go through my meagre luggage.

At Bordeaux my former companions left me, to hurry on to their respective destinations, and I was alone, very much a stranger in a strange land. Everything looked odd to my New England eyes—the stone houses and stores, the roughly paved streets, and the people, with whom I had no means of holding conversation. It all engendered a peculiarly helpless feeling in me, and this increased as I began to realize that the passers-by were recognizing me as an American and smiling pleasantly.

The address of my hotel—the *De Bayonne*—had been written for me on a slip of paper, and this I handed to a cab-man outside the dock. He nodded, slung my duffle bag and grip aboard his rickety hack, and I followed them.

When we arrived at the hotel I asked him, in English, of course, what the tax might be. He doubtless guessed my meaning; but that was more than I could do when he answered, of course in French; so I handed him a five *franc* note (I had changed my American money on ship-board). My jehu laboriously counted out about a handful of strange-looking chicken-feed as my change and, not knowing what a proper tip would be, I compromised by handing it all back to him. He seemed satisfied.

19

The Hotel de Bayonne was small, but astonished me by its elaborate and almost gorgeous decorations, and I soon found that it held an excellent restaurant, for this was the first thing that I visited. By following the simple method of pointing at items near the top, middle and bottom of the menu I obtained a very fair meal of soup, veal, lentils, bread and the ever-present "*confiture*"—a sort of jam, without which no self-respecting French meal is complete—and red wine.

As the pangs of hunger began to be appeased I paid more attention to my neighbours, many of whom were fascinatingly pretty French girls, with merry lips and languishing dark eyes. And I could not talk French! Right then I resolved to master the language at once.

In the hotel was a man who had charge of shipping my ilk to Paris, and he gave me my ticket and directions for finding the depot, where an electric sign pointed me to the right train. No seats or berths (it was now evening) were to be obtained, so, lonesome enough, I stood in the aisle for a while, and finally took a couple of blankets from my duffle bag and went to sleep on the floor. It seemed quite warlike.

At seven the following morning we reached the city with the magic name, and, following the old procedure, I took a taxicab to the headquarters of the Harjes-Norton Ambulance Corps, to report my arrival.

CHAPTER 2

A Soldier of the Legion

The very first person whom I met there, standing in the doorway, was a tall, blond chap who somehow looked mightily familiar. He turned out to be none other than the son of my Latin professor back in High School days—the only man who could make me behave, and that merely by a patient, troubled look. His name was Phil Davis, and perhaps I was not glad to see a countryman and an old neighbour! [1] Abroad, any one from the same city is a neighbour, of course.

We chatted for some few moments. He told me that he had gone over in the ambulance service and shifted to aviation—all the red-blooded men were doing it now, he said.

That was the last straw; *I* determined to shift immediately.

Davis also spoke a serious word about the real war situation, and began to open my eyes to the truth, and the desperate need of France. The impression which his words made upon my mind was reflected in a letter that I wrote home to mother a few days later, and in which I told her what I had done.

Why, mother, we (at home) don't realize the seriousness of this war. France is almost wiped out, and they are 'playing on their nerve.' Most of their wonderful men and boys are gone. England has started, but many claim that if we had not come to the rescue when we did, the Germans would have won the war inside of six months. Their fighting ability and their cruelty cannot be described. They are devils, and unless appearances are

1. Philip W. Davis, to whom Sergeant Wellman gives much of the credit for his own enlistment in the aviation service and who was one of the three boys from Newton, Massachusetts, who figure in this story, was later transferred to the American Army as a lieutenant, and was reported to have been shot down behind the German lines and killed on June second.—The Original Editor.

mighty deceitful they will be able to hold out for a long while.
. . . There is nothing in the world that Our Country should not
do for France at this time.

The words spoken by Davis drove the last rivet in my resolve. I
said that I meant to follow suit, and he briefly outlined the necessary
procedure.

I went at once into the office and, after reporting to Mr. Norton's
brother there, told him of my desire and determination. He was all
kindness and released me from my former contract.

Without delay I found my way to 23 Avenue Bois de Bologne,
where I found Dr. Edmund Gros, a distinguished-looking man of
middle years, with graying hair and a close clipped moustache, who
was in charge of the Paris enlistments in the Lafayette Flying Corps.
He greeted me warmly when I introduced myself and explained my
reason for visiting him.

After Dr. Gros had read my letters of recommendation, which I
had wisely brought along with me, he said that if I passed the physical
examination, which I should return to take that afternoon, he would
accept me. I lunched at a nearby restaurant, but, having heard something of the severity of the tests given our would-be aviators at home,
was too excited over the prospect to eat a great deal.

Then, after a brief walk through the unfamiliar streets, I returned
to Dr. Gros's office. It was not long before I had learned that the
French and American examinations, given prospective flyers, were
quite different things. When a thug is pounding at one's very doors,
the owner of the house does not stop to search for his latest model
automatic pistol, but grabs whatever he can lay his hands on to beat
off the intruder. That was the case with France. She was not spending
months in developing the most theoretically perfect airplane, or in
securing and training men who were theoretically the best qualified
to run it. Rather her motto was *"get men and machines into the air as
quickly as possible."*

History will write the story of the results.

So it was that my examination was simple in the extreme. It merely
consisted of heart tests, after I had hopped about the floor a few times;
eye tests by reading a few letters across the room; balancing on one
foot with my eyes closed to prove that I had a fair sense of equilibrium; and a few other balancing tests, during which I was whirled
around on a piano stool with eyes closed and then requested to walk a

22

straight line, *with them open*. Weight and measurements followed, and it was all over, and I was pronounced physically fit for the aerial service of the historic French Foreign Legion, of which the Lafayette Flying Corps was a part.

Dr. Gros had told me to return to my hotel, the *France et Choiseul* on Rue St. Honoré, and wait for my enlistment papers from the French government. I waited for two weeks, with my impatience growing daily, and, although I found plenty to do and see in order to make the time pass pleasantly, I sometimes felt that the American motto of "DO IT *NOW*" had never been translated into French. In my own estimation, my enlistment was quite the most important thing in the immediate carrying on of the war.

However, from time to time, I gained a little inside information on what was before me, as I became acquainted with men belonging to the corps who happened to be in Paris on permission, whom I recognized by their uniform and spoke to.

The thirteenth of June produced an incident notable in my enforced stay. It was no less than the arrival in Paris of that great American general over whose splendid troops of the Rainbow Division I was one day to be flying, although I did not guess it then.

He came alone, save for a few members of his staff, being in France merely to look over the ground, so the papers said; but, if he had brought an army of a million men, instead of the mere promise, his reception could not possibly have been more madly enthusiastic. The afternoon editions of the papers carried in big type the announcement of his impending arrival, and an invitation to the populace to turn out and greet him royally. They did.

Almost every day something occurred, or some band of heroes returned, to create a burst of truly Latin excitement, but at no time, there or elsewhere, have I ever heard an ovation such as was given General Pershing as he rode in an open carriage with Minister Painleve through the Grande Boulevard, followed by one containing Marshall Joffre—the idol of the French—and the American Ambassador Sharpe.

Paris simply went wild. The streets were jammed and the crowds pushed forward only to be pushed back again by the dapper little *gendarmes*. Men and women laughed and shouted with joy. They, who had borne three years of anguish with the most wonderful fortitude, stood and watched him pass, the tears streaming down their faces. Little children threw him kisses and strewed flowers in the streets. His carriage was filled with blossoms.

And this acclaim was all for just one man who had, as yet, done nothing; but the people sensed what he was going to do. By George, I felt proud and happy to be an American!

"Papa" Joffre came in for an ovation scarcely less jubilant, and why not?

He had been their saviour in the time of their first dire need, just as Pershing promised to be now, and he represented the very acme of French military prowess and achievement. What a man he looked, with his massive head and white hair; but I could not help feeling that Pershing, thin, hard as iron, bronzed almost to the colour of an Indian by wind and weather, and with his firm-set lips and bristling gray moustache, looked even more like the real fighter.

If this were a story of travel merely, I might add several more interesting and amusing things about my first experiences among the new sights and sensations that Paris offers one who visits her for the first time. But it is not, so I shall record only two of peculiar personal interest—the one growing out of the other.

I discovered that one of the hotel valets—a short but powerfully built little chap—had some skill with his hands, and one morning was having a friendly bout with him, *en negligé*, for I have always loved to box.

Somehow, I cut my foot slightly and, with my customary carelessness, paid no attention to the wound. The next day I found that it was suppurating and I recognized the signs of blood poisoning, for I nearly lost the same leg from that disease a few years before after an injury received playing baseball.

I went at once to see Dr. Gros, and, to my great disgust, for I was daily expecting my enlistment papers, he insisted that I go for treatment to the American Hospital at Nueilly, outside of Paris. I had to obey, of course, and soon became reconciled to it, for my foot was in pretty bad shape, and the nurses from home were very nice. In fact, the hospital was a wonderfully attractive, homelike place with its American Red Cross doctors, nurses and food, and the care that I received was of the best. Three square Yankee meals a day certainly seemed good to me, and at times I almost regretted that I should soon have to exchange them for the "*poilu*" rations served at Avord, concerning which I had heard much, and nothing good, from my chance acquaintances.

I was put to bed in a cheerful, immaculately white ward, with six other banged up chaps, all of whom had been injured in training or in the ambulance service.

There I stayed seven long days, to be discharged as practically cured, on June the twenty-third, by which time I was feeling as fit as the proverbial fiddle, although the doctor told me to go lightly on my foot for awhile.

One of my recently made acquaintances at the hotel was "Doc" Cookson from Chicago. That afternoon he came for me in a taxi and we drove to Paris. When we reached the Seine, on the outskirts of the Metropolis proper, we decided to dismiss our vehicle and stroll slowly in along the river's bank.

We had progressed only a few steps along the broad sidewalk on the steep concrete embankment, when I saw a pale, distracted looking young girl, clad in the black uniform of a street car conductress, run to the railing, climb it and, before I could make a move, she had thrown herself with a ringing shriek headlong into the river beneath.

Her act was so sudden that for an instant I scarcely realized what she meant to do. Then, with no thought for my foot, I ran to the spot whence she had disappeared. She had not come to the surface. Cookson said that he could not swim, and the crowd of excited Frenchmen that speedily collected either could not or would not, so it seemed to be up to me.

In a few seconds I had stripped off my outer clothing and shoes, and dived into what seemed to me to be the dirtiest water in the world. It was perhaps a dozen feet deep at the spot. I would go down, grope blindly along the oozy mud of the bottom, come up to fill my lungs, and dive again into that liquid murkiness. For fully fifteen minutes I kept this up, driven on, not by any hope of saving the poor girl's life, but by an unwillingness to quit, until I was almost exhausted.

By that time Cookson and some *gendarmes* had secured a rope, grappling hooks and a boat.

For some minutes more we tried to locate the body, and at last succeeded. She was dead, of course.

That night I did not sleep a great deal, for that shriek, the white, wan face and stringy, dripping hair, and especially the thought that I had been almost exactly on the spot and yet had failed to save her life, haunted my thoughts when awake and my sleeping dreams.

Incidentally I spoiled a good suit of clothes, and opened the cut in my foot and its physical pain added to my mental discomfort.

Still, the return to the hotel had produced one cheering bit of news. My papers had come, and I had the satisfaction of realizing that I was actually a Soldier of France. To be sure, it was only second class, which made me the recipient of the princely salary of twenty-five *centimes* (*five cents*) a day. For an American to live on any such amount, even with "board and lodging" thrown in, was, of course, impossible; but I knew that, through the generosity of Mr. William K. Vanderbilt, the Godfather of the Lafayette Corps,[2] I would receive the additional amount of two hundred *francs* (forty dollars) a month.

It was not the money that interested me then, however. Every day had added something to my knowledge of the critical condition of France and the allied armies, and of the crying need for men, especially in the air, where the war must be won—if we can believe Lord Kitchener, who had once said that one airplane was worth three thousand infantrymen,

I had read every bit of news regarding the doings home—or rather had it read to me, for my knowledge of French was still in the rudimentary state,—and in a letter to my mother, dated June twenty-sixth, I wrote, "By Jove, we are certainly getting ahead. That wonderful air fleet that America has planned is what we need!" I left France nearly a year later, and had not seen any of it!

On the twenty-seventh of June I went to the headquarters of the Foreign Legion and took my oath of enlistment for the duration of the war, and that afternoon boarded the train southward bound for the training camp at Avord.

I was alone at the outset; but soon made the acquaintance of two Americans on board, Joseph Stehlen, of New York, who had been in training there four months and was returning after a brief leave, spent (as it always is) in Paris, and a chap named Whitmore, from Philadelphia, who had been laid up in the hospital, having broken his leg and injured his eye by falling in his machine while flying.

They appointed themselves my bodyguard, and not only smoothed the way for me at meal time, for they both spoke French fluently, but told me many things about what I might expect in camp.

It was nine o'clock and fairly dusk when we arrived at the little depot which bore the name of Avord. There was no town, the district being a farming one, but a third—or worse—rate hotel and some half a dozen provision stores and restaurants clustered about the station.

Several motor trucks, or lorries, from the school were waiting, and we embarked in one of them for the drive out to the field.

2. *The Story of the Lafayette Escadrille* by Georges Thenault also published by Leonaur.

26

My first impressions of my new home? I had none. I was crowded in between a huge pile of bags and boxes, the road was so rough that I jounced every inch of the way, and my foot ached like the mischief.

At last we drew up at a big gate, set in a twelve-foot wooden fence which extended to right and left, to be lost in the darkness and which, in fact, enclosed several fields so huge that it took an automobile an hour and a half to circle it, as I discovered later.

A sentry opened the gate to let us pass in, and we were driven up to a long row of white shed-like barracks dimly lighted by oil lamps. Before them I saw a considerable number of men standing and sitting about. They were obviously Americans, and regarded me curiously.

Just as I climbed lamely out of the conveyance, a tall, broad-shouldered lad, with a frank, open countenance, crowned with blond hair that stuck out "all ways for Sunday," came running out of one of the doors.

I stood stock still and stared at him, and he returned the compliment. The next instant we were gripping hands with mutual exclamations of surprise and delight. It was "Dave" Putnam, since become one of the most famous of American aces. He was a *real* neighbour of the old days at home in Newton, and a lad with whom I had gone through High School, and behind whose sturdy back in the football line I had given signals thousands of times.

I had not known that he was at Avord, and he had not known that I was coming.

Dave immediately constituted himself my guide, and took me to the commissary depot, half a mile distant, to get my bed. The word certainly sounded attractive, but I cannot say as much for the thing that it represented. It consisted of two wooden horses, a narrow wooden platform, and an evil-appearing straw mattress which looked as though it might be fairly alive. It was!

There was no superior present to tell me what I should do or where I should go, so I picked out the only vacant spot in the bunkhouse, occupied by Dave and a dozen others, and set up my bed between those of two men who were introduced to me as Buckley (he is now a prisoner in Germany) and Dan Huger, who later developed heart trouble when at the front and had to go home.

As it was now ten o'clock and after, and I was dog tired, I slid into my blankets and tried to go to sleep. "*Tried*" is used advisedly, for my first night as a Soldier of the Legion was one of disillusionment.

CHAPTER 3

Back in School

On Monday, the twenty-eighth day of June, I awoke—no, I was awakened—to a realization that it was still pitchy black out-of-doors. My night had been a restless one, sleep having visited me only at intervals between attacks from above and beneath, for the bunk house was full of flies, and the mattress filled with many creeping things of different species whose names are not mentioned in polite society. To anticipate, I may say that, before long, I became an acknowledged expert in diagnosing bites made by them, and "Show it to Wellman," was often heard when someone discovered a peculiar looking wound. Also that I could come pretty near guessing the length of the rat who had strolled, with clammy feet, across my face during the night.

I sat up in the dim light, rubbed my eyes, and saw a couple of dozen other fellows doing the same. Only one of them, Putnam, was known to me; but I was soon to know all the rest nearly as intimately, for a small bunk house, the same tasks, "eats," pleasures and discomforts, make for close fellowship.

We were all Americans there, although within the school were hundreds of Frenchmen, not to mention Russians, Italians and Portuguese; we were all in the service of France; we were all bound together by mutual aims and mutual interests; we were all on one plane of democratic equality—but what a variety we would have represented if suddenly transplanted back into civilian life! The old rhyme of *Doctor, lawyer, beggarman, thief*, would have fallen far short of describing us adequately.

In that one barrack was everything from millionaires to prize fighters. The last-mentioned class was represented by a man whom I shall not name, because, at last reports, he was viewing the walls of a military prison from the wrong side; but he was certainly an expert in his ex-profession, and although I considered myself a pretty fair boxer, he laid me cold more than once, in rainy day bouts.

This is, perhaps, as good a place as any to introduce to you some of those companions of mine with whom I lived, flew and finally fought, although they were not all represented that morning. Some were quartered in other barracks, some came to the school later.

Foremost among them, as far as general public interest is concerned, was Jules Baylies of New Bedford, America's greatest ace at the time of his death or capture, early last June. The reason for his subsequent successes was obvious during his Avord training, for, even as a young *pilote*, he kept our hair on end by performing the wildest possible stunts in the air, with the nonchalance of a born aviator. The war was no new thing to him, for he had, prior to shifting over into aviation, driven an ambulance all over the western front, and earned the "*Croix de Guerre*" for conspicuous bravery in that service.

Tall, brawny, dark-haired and good-looking, he was a typical Yankee athlete-soldier, and his record in the school earned him the distinguished honour of being assigned to the "Stork" Escadrille of the French service, a member of which, the immortal Guynemer, was killed after strafing fifty-two Hun planes. That *escadrille* always flew in the most active sector.

Most popular of all was Reginald Sinclair, whom I have already described, together with the reason for his popularity. We trained together from start to finish and went to the front at the same time, his station being the *escadrille* located just to the left of mine. At the time of this writing Sinclair has got only two official planes; but he is still in the game, and with luck, is due to boost his score materially, for he is an excellent *pilote*. As an illustration of the "luck" of this game, take the case of Major Thaw, the most wonderful flyer with the Lafayette Escadrille, and one of our biggest aces, yet he did his work perfectly for almost three years, and had only one Boche to his credit, before his big "run" started.

The man who, perhaps, typified the general spirit of the school more than any other was Austin B. Crehore, of New York, who was with me throughout the training at Avord, Pau and at Plessis Belleville later. He was far from robust physically, and all the time was suffering intermittently from chronic appendicitis. Again and again one of the other men and I had to help him home to the barracks from the flying field, half carrying him; undress him and put him to bed, he was suffering so. But he stuck like a bulldog, reached the front and, during

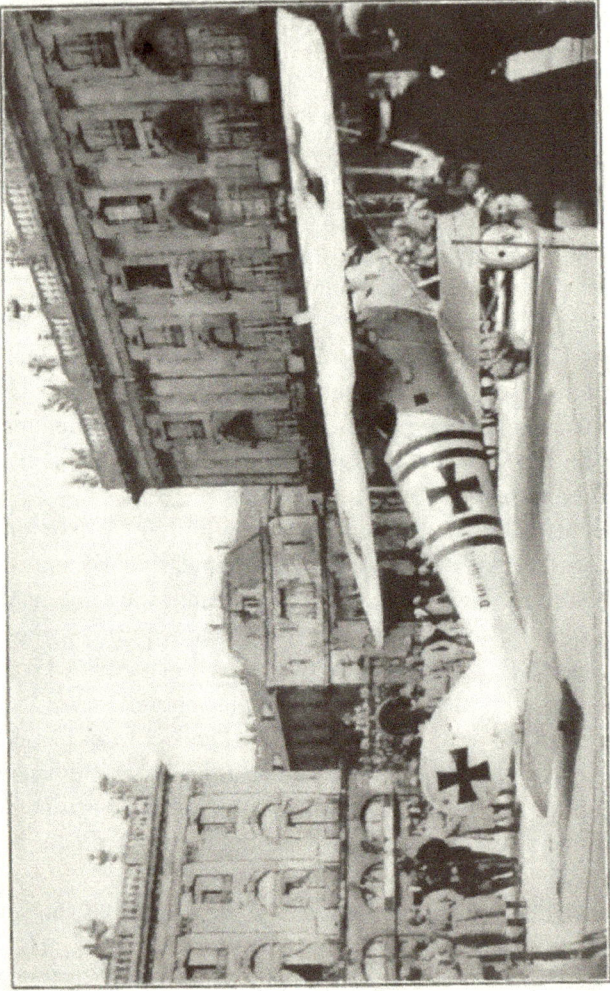

SINCLAIR'S FIRST VICTIM

each of his first three weeks of fighting, brought down a Boche. Then, and not until then, did he feel that he had earned a rest, and he went to the hospital and had his troublesome appendix out.

Another highly popular chap was Tom Potter of New York, who had driven an ambulance on the French, Italian and Serbian fronts before changing over. He was a wonderful pianist, and, since he had a "box" in his room, it was a popular meeting place.

Dave Putnam after his "graduation" was sent to the Champaigne sector, and I met him only occasionally on leaves, but he was another splendid *pilote* and quickly started in to make a big name in the game.[3]

Those of you who are especially interested in bicycling have doubtless read the name of "Egg," the great French racer. We had an "Egg," too—or rather an "Egg" Drew. His given name was "Sidney, Jr.," and he was the son of the ever popular stage and motion picture actor. The title was bestowed upon him in derision after he had purchased no less than three bicycles, not one of which would work. After a splendid record at the front poor Drew was shot down and killed in the Spring of this year.

Among the others were Blumenthal, the famous Princeton centre and guard—news of whose shooting down are in the papers as I am writing this; Mosely, the Yale end; David Judd, of Brookline, Massachusetts; Ollie Chadwick, the Harvard football star; Wally Winter, of Chicago; Tom Buffum, Don Stone and Louhran, Taylor and Benny who have made the final great sacrifice. All these names, and those of others who will be mentioned in this brief history, have appeared often in print the past year and I will not stop to describe them.

But one other must be mentioned at this time, for he was to become my closest and most trusted comrade through fair weather and foul for several months, until, shot down in combat with five Hun machines, wounded and taken prisoner, his flying days ended, for a time at least.

This was "Tommy" Hitchcock, the seventeen-year-old son of Ma-

---

3. Early in May Sergeant Wellman's friend, David E. Putnam, downed his fifth Boche, which made him an "Ace," and on the same day a sixth, for which achievements the French government bestowed upon him the "*Medaille Militare,*" he having already won the "*Croix de Guerre.*" Subsequently he accounted for two more, and early in June, after having been transferred to the American service with the rank of first lieutenant, he gained the remarkable distinction of bringing down *five enemy's machines in one day.* This raised his official record to thirteen, and made him the American "Ace of Aces."—The Original Editor.

Lieutenant David E. Putnam

jor Thomas H. Hitchcock, of Westbury, L. I., and the Mineola Aviation School, who was before the war a famous polo player.

Tom was the baby of the school in years, but in all things else he reached the measure of a *man*. Although he was so young he was splendidly built, with the muscles of a trained athlete, and such, indeed, he was, having made his mark on the polo field, tennis court and other places where sports are held, when he was in short trousers. He was a blond, good looking and good company, and "clean"—mentally, morally and physically.

Tom arrived at Avord a month after I did, we "chummed up" immediately and, although I had a head start in training, I reached the front only a little in advance of him; in fact, he established a speed record for Americans in going through the course.

So much for a brief caste of the principal characters, who were to play out the daily drama and comedy of school life in our barracks. Now to return to the story.

Before my bunk stood "Jimmie," and Jimmie was quite the queerest looking biped I had ever laid eyes upon—a sort of cross between an Indo and a Chinaman, with a little dash of characteristic unlike either, in short, an Annamede from the French oriental province of Annam. He spoke neither French nor English, and the only language that was mutually understandable was the profane. At this he was highly proficient, and I found that almost nightly he received a lesson, for he would stand grinning in the centre of the floor and repeat, parrotlike, the bad words shouted at him by those he served.

Jimmie bore a large wooden bucket of inky appearing liquid which masqueraded under the name of coffee. Heaven knows what was in it, but when I tasted it I found that it was strong enough to have waked the dead. And bitter! We used to sit on the edge of our beds and hang onto the side of them while we gulped it down. Still, it was a wonderful eye-opener.

Following the example of my new companions, I made haste into my clothes, which were still those of a civilian, for the hour was getting late (it was almost three-thirty!) and sunrise ought to find us on the field. The hours of early morning and those of eveningtide are the best for flying, especially in the summer, for there is then likely to be less wind, and less of the fluky air conditions which the heat of noonday produces.

As bad as the bed had been, I looked a bit longingly at the blankets which I had just quitted, for I found that I was still lame and tired.

"Hurry up," someone shouted. "We've got to be on the march in fifteen minutes, and you'd better dress warmly. It will be pretty chilly for a few hours, although hotter than Hades by noon."

"Breakfast . . .?" I began.

There was a general laugh. "Breakfast! What kind of a Frenchman are you? Come on, no time to shave." (A little later all the Americans, on a bet, went without shaving for two months, and we were a wild looking bunch.)

I followed the rest out into the half light and felt the ghostly touch of the night mists on my face. We formed a semi-military line and marched out to the first field, twenty minutes' distant. The sky brightened momentarily, first a mere tawny rift appearing in the mist, then a yellow tinge spread over everything and the fog disappeared to give place to the glowing colours of dawn.

We approached the hangars of the *Blériot* school. These, as you may know, are like immense, oblong circus tents with curved roofs, made of canvas stretched over a wooden framework, their sides ten or a dozen feet high, backs enclosed, and fronts covered with canvas flaps. Already monitors (instructors) were arriving, and the mechanics were busy pulling the flaps back and wheeling out the machines, immense darning needles. Some of the men climbed into theirs on orders from the head instructor, and began to test their motors and the air was torn to shreds by the deafening banging and clattering, above the incessant racket of which I could scarcely hear myself think. It quieted down at last and up came running a dapper little Frenchman who I learned was De Rungé. As he arrived he called out, in English, "Good morning, American bums." (Someone had told him that this was a polite greeting, and he believed it!)

There was a general laugh, instantly stilled when he began to call out briskly, in French, "Putnam, take machine number thirty-five," and so on, until all but I were placed.

At another command the mechanics spun the several propellers, and the racket began again. The assistants pulled away the blocks from beneath the pair of small wheels on each machine, and soon the rosy eastern sky was filled with high darting black specks—the more advanced birdmen; the nearer air with the fledglings; while the ground bore still more, taxiing about and looking like fish out of water.

Everywhere were monitors, pupil aviators of various classes, mechanics and labourers, all as busy as bees and with no time to pay any attention to a newcomer.

34

I tried to eat a piece of the dark, heavy and bitter war bread and soft, wormy cheese that was laid out in a camion near the hangars, but found no appetite for it, and then stood around for a few moments, watching the animated scene with a good deal of the eagerness of a small boy on a back lot, who wants to be invited to join a game of "scrub"; for, as one machine after another taxied past me with a clatter and whirr, and then slid smoothly into the air, my blood started pounding with the mad joy of anticipation.

At length I asked someone to direct me to the commanding officer, and he pointed out a small, thickset and nattily dressed officer, who stood watching the field with snapping black eyes, meanwhile curling a little pointed black moustache. It was Capitaine Terrio, in charge of the first three classes.

I approached him, performed what was my conception of a military salute, and reported that I was one of his new pupils.

If I had cherished any idea that he would be so glad to get me that he would welcome me with open arms and kiss me French style, it was quickly dissipated, for all that he did was to snap out in a businesslike manner, "What's your name?"

I told him, and he continued, "Very good. Report immediately to Sergeant Parrisoy, of the first class."

With another salute I turned away, and finally succeeded in locating the sergeant, only to be told that the class was then full and that I would have to await my turn. I waited, wild with impatience to be up and doing, for four days; but in the interim somewhat accustomed myself to the manners and customs of the place.

While waiting for my turn to come, and then proceeding with the chronological sequence of events, I will briefly describe the salient features of my life during the months which were to follow, so that you may have the complete setting.

Here, then, are two samples, taken from the stock of summer days—one blue and one gray.

I have already pictured the start of a day and in this respect they were all alike. In the early summer it was a case of getting up before three, for, if the weather were fair, we were supposed to be in our planes—either on the ground or in the air—from sunrise until nine o'clock, at which hour we returned to the barracks.

Then we had the time to ourselves until about five in the afternoon, and before dinner, which was served at one o'clock, we would loaf or lie on our beds and essay the impossible—*i.e.*, to get to sleep, for the days were often hotter than the devil's kitchen. As a matter of fact the time was more often spent in a never-ending battle against flies, big and little, and bugs, little and big, and at one time or another during the day you might have seen a row of us, stripped to the waist and industriously picking them from our undershirts, or burning them out of the seams with automatic cigar lighters. A jack-knife blade run down a crack anywhere in the bunkhouse would do wholesale murder.

By dinner time I was always ravenously hungry, but my appetite often went back on me when the food was set out on the rough board table in the building, three minutes' walk distant, which served as a dining hall. Almost invariably it was horse meat, tough and gamey, lentils which contained many little pebbles so completely camouflaged that I found it easier to swallow them than to search them out, *real* war bread, and coffee.

If I did not wholly relish the rations, the flies did, and always favoured us with their company in swarms.

The afternoon was a duplication of the morning, with, perhaps, the interpolation of a game of cards, dice or *baseball*, for early in July one of our officers, who had heard a good deal about the great American national pastime, and never seen it played, suggested that we make up two teams and give an exhibition.

There were several excellent players in the camp—old college and school stars—but not enough to make two evenly balanced teams. Nevertheless we succeeded in putting up a pretty fast brand of ball, and the Frenchmen immediately went wild over it and came in crowds to every game. We played three times a week.

The honour of captaining one of the nines was thrust upon me, and my team managed to pull off the greater number of victories during the series.

At five o'clock we were back at the *piste*, or flying field, and ready to continue the afternoon session until it was too dark to see, which might mean as late as nine-thirty.

Supper, a second edition of dinner, followed, and then, until bed time, which, tired as we were, was generally postponed like most unpleasant things, we amused ourselves with games, or by watching the Annamedes and half-naked black Arabian *zouaves* perform their native dances about camp fires in their quarters, to the unsymphonic accompaniment of weird crooning and the thumping of *tom-toms*. The dances were as sinuous and sensuous as any Hawaiian *hula-hula*, and, with the ruddy firelight reflected on the dusky and ebony bodies, the effect was outlandish in the extreme. Moreover, they used an intoxicating native drug, and the dance often ended in a fight.

This, except for the interpolation of special incidents, is an accurate, but sketchy, pen picture of our every-day existence, when the weather was fit for flying.

Rain, and there was a lot of it, or impossible flying conditions brought an intermixture of feelings. It gave us a vacation which we generally needed, but it also retarded our progress, and, as we were all eager to get to the front and actually into the fight, every delay was maddening.

On such days we would have roll-call in the early morning, and then be dismissed, to spend the time according to our own sweet will.

Most fortunately for us we had what we called our "clubhouse." It was a little stone farmhouse not far from the field, which a motherly little French woman of the peasant type, slender, bent and weather-beaten, had taken early in the summer, and ran with the aid of two sisters. What her real name was I never knew; but we called her "Old Mammy," and a mammy she was to us all.

Old Mammy kept her own cow and chickens and provided us with real "home" cooking,—of the French kind, of course.

This establishment was truly a God-send to us Americans, and we would troop thither at every opportunity to spend on decent food, the "pin money" thoughtfully supplied by Mr. Vanderbilt. We had the run of the place, and in the low ceilinged, tile-floored room which served as a combination living- and dining-room, we had a tin-pany piano, and sang, smoked, played cards, threw dice and boxed as the spirit moved.

Is it any wonder that we frequented such a truly delightful place as often as possible, especially when we could there purchase for two *francs*-fifty (fifty cents) real breakfasts of a couple of eggs, toast with butter and fresh milk, and other meals far better than the French government was able to supply us with? And is it any wonder that I was perpetually broke?

CHAPTER 4

Flying: on the Ground and in the Air

On the first day of July I received my initiation into the intricacies of flying. It was, however, like a person learning to swim on dry land, or the case of a baby who has to learn to crawl before he can walk.

At that time the French were training their aviators by the "rule of thumb." We had no preliminary schooling in the theories of aeronautics, study of the construction of the planes, preliminary flights with a teacher or military drill, as in America. They tried a drill one day, but it was not a howling success and was never repeated.

"There's your plane; if you do so and so, such and such a thing will happen; get into it and go to it."

That is a brief summary of the method of instruction then pursued at Avord, although I understand that it has since been somewhat changed. It was a modern version of the old Spartan "survival of the fittest" manner of raising children; *but it turned out real flyers.*

Not, of course, that we "went aloft" the first day, or for many days, the ground class being the, longest and most tedious of all.

I was introduced to my first machine, and when I climbed aboard I felt as proud as a boy with a new bicycle, for, although it was merely a sadly battered old *Blériot*, it represented to me the first step toward a much desired end. Of course, being a *Blériot*, it was a one-seated monoplane—that is, it had single wings, and their normal spread had been reduced to twelve metres (thirty-six feet approximately) by clipping. It would not leave the ground, and accordingly the nickname applied to this type of machine—a "Penguin"—is obviously appropriate.

Since it is my desire to write this chapter rather for the reader who is wholly unversed in the theories of flying than for you who understand at least its rudiments, I will give a few simple explanations here.

The monoplane machines of the types that I flew, were all very

38

lightly constructed of slender pieces of spruce, covered with canvas, and that is the usual construction, although some of the big three-place planes—like the one that killed Luffberry—are lightly armored. The long, tapering body is called the *fuselage*. At the front, just below the wings, is the cockpit and seat for the pilot, and, in front of him, is the engine, whose two-bladed, wooden propeller *draws* the machine through the air, except in the heavy *Voison* plane, in which the engine is behind the operator, and the propeller *pushes* it forward, as does the screw of a steamship.

At the back of the *fuselage* are two rudders which work independently, one vertical, and the other horizontal and each divided into two parts. The latter are called the rear ailerons, or elevators, and are connected by wires to the *manche à balai*, or control stick, which comes up between the pilot's extended legs. When this is pulled backward, the rear *ailerons* are elevated and cause the nose of the machine to point upward, and when it is drawn back the opposite results. Other wires connect the control stick to the ends of the wings.

In the *Blériot* and *Caudron* types the wings are warped, and in most others the wires operate hinged flaps called the side *ailerons*. When the control stick is moved sideways to the right, the *aileron* on the left hand wing is lifted, and that on the right hand one dropped, which causes the machine to tilt downward on the right hand side, and of course the opposite result is obtained by moving the stick to the left. The vertical rudder, which steers the plane's course exactly after the manner of a boat, is worked by a very simple device like that on a double runner sled, a narrow piece of wood operated by the pilot's feet. So much for a very simple description of an airplane.

Of course I had no need to worry about any of the controls but the last mentioned, during my training in the first class, the purpose of which was merely to teach the pupil how to control his engine,—in my case a thirty-five horse power, stationary three-cylinder Anzani radial motor—and steer a straight course, with the *fuselage* horizontal, for half a mile down the field.

This running the plane straight across the field sounds simple, doesn't it? Well, it is not—for the beginner, at least,—and it is a fact that the customary length of time spent in learning to do this one thing properly, at Avord, was a full month. Some took a longer and some a shorter period, and the same is true of all the subsequent "stunts," so it is obvious that "classes" had no fixed graduation day.

Sergeant Parrisoy told me briefly what my stunt was to be, and how to perform it—one of the other fellows interpreting, for it was many weeks before I knew enough French to get along without friendly assistance from a go-between. I got set confidently. A mechanic was called to give my propeller a twirl, which was the method of cranking the engine, I gave her the gas and the spark, and was off.

If you have ever seen an intoxicated man stagger waveringly down the sidewalk, just missing bumping into posts and people, you can mentally picture my progress, for first I pressed too much on one side, then on the other, of my foot-tiller. Eventually I reached my destination, the other side of the long field; but, if my course had been charted, the result would certainly not have served as a geometric diagram proving that the shortest distance between two points is a straight line.

I improved steadily, however, and, although the daily task was one highly conducive to the use of profanity, for it seemed as though I were getting nowhere fast, three weeks after my maiden trip I actually heard my teacher say the heart-gladdening words, "Wellman, tomorrow you may go into the second class."

During these three weeks two events of particular interest to me happened. First I got my uniform—a dark blue, close fitting tunic with open collar and a single row of steel buttons, bearing a winged propeller blade, and trousers of the same colour, with a hair line of orange down the outer seams. That day I strutted about inwardly prouder than any general in the French army with his gold lace and insignia.

The other occurred when I witnessed the first demonstration of the truth of the axiom that luck plays the leading part in flying.

One evening, early in July, a number of us were standing around at the *piste*, as the aviation field was called, having completed our day's work, and were watching the real flyers come in and alight, one by one. At last our attention was attracted to one machine flying low over the little cluster of buildings about the Avord depot, and, as we watched it, we saw it suddenly swoop down and disappear straight through the roof of one of them.

Capitaine Terrio and several others, among whom I was one, ran for a nearby automobile, and broke all speed records over the half mile of horribly rough road that separated our field from the site of the accident, which we fully believed had resulted in a fatality.

When we arrived, the first thing which our eyes fell upon was the flaming auburn hair of "Red" Scanlon, as he stood at salute in the doorway of the bakery which he had "just dropped into" while passing.

Although he was covered with mortar dust there was scarcely a scratch on him, despite the fact that his plane had gone through the roof until only its rudder stuck out, and had been smashed to smithereens. He told us that his motor had stopped dead, just as he was about to end his flight home, and that his momentum had not been sufficient to carry him clear of the buildings.

Yes, nerve, judgement and experience are three highly important factors in flying; but pure luck tops them all.

Therefore it is hardly strange that aviators are highly superstitious, and that almost every one carries some mascot on which he pins his faith. At just about this time I wrote home in haste for something to act as my charm, selecting a photograph of my mother and one of "the girl I left behind me" in a leather folder, and I carried this close to my heart throughout my whole career in France, with what effect you shall hear later.

Promotion to the second class sounded like a real step forward; but it really meant ten days more of the same sort of terrestrial trips, this time in a *Blériot* of the Rolleur type, with full sized wings, but with its six-cylinder motor throttled down to half speed, so that the machine could not leave the earth for its real habitat in the air.

Unlike the *"Penguin"* which bumped over the ground like a light weight automobile, this machine had a buoyancy that caused it to skim along so that the sensation of the pilot was the next thing to actual flying. It also responded much more easily to the rudder.

The feeling engendered in me was indescribably odd as I went whizzing along, barely touching the ground. It was not to be compared with that which was to come later, hurtling through space; but more like the one which you may have had yourself, if you have ever found yourself walking unconcernedly in the air in your dreams. It gripped me so that I left my machine with regret at night and eagerly anticipated the next "go" at it.

Again, this period brought one occurrence which is still strongly outstanding in my memory. I had seen death before, but never one of violence. It happened one evening,—a peaceful, quiet twilight night which made the thought of tragedy remote. Most of the machines were safe on land, but two *Voison* planes—big two-seated affairs in which a *quartette* of French students were learning the gentle art of bombing—were still on high. Just what happened to one of them we never knew; but, when both were over the field, it apparently went out of control, and rammed the other at full speed. There was a crash, as they collided in midair, their wings crumpled up as though made of pasteboard, and down they fell, tumbling over and over in a mass of flames, for the gasoline tank of each must have been smashed, and the *essence* immediately ignited.

We ran for the spot where they landed, but too late to accomplish anything. All four men, and both machines, had been burned to a cinder.

Once more I passed a troubled night. A fellow cannot help but wonder, after witnessing such a tragedy, if he will himself someday be the victim of a similar one, even though he may know that the chances are all in his favour, and that fewer accidents occur in airplanes than in automobiles.

While I was at Avord, the American students were extremely fortunate, and not one was killed and few injured, although some of other nationalities were less lucky.

Then came the last of July, and my promotion to the class which spelled the real thing, flying twenty-five feet off the ground.

A child on Christmas eve, with his mind full of what Santa Claus is going to bring him on the morrow, might serve as an example of me the night after I received word of my promotion into the air, and I tried my best to form some mental impression of the sensation that I was to experience when I, too, became one of the birdmen who sailed off the ground so gracefully, sported around in the ether with perfect ease, and then softly slid to earth down an invisible slope.

The field where the third class held forth was much further from the barracks, it taking nearly three-quarters of an hour to reach in a tractor truck, or *camion*.

When the morning was about to dawn I heard one of my companions call, "Hurry all everybody, the *camion* leaves in fifteen minutes and if you miss it, it's a case of a long, long trail on foot to the field." With eager anticipation I hurried into my clothes, and outside. The *camion* was waiting, and Annamedes were piling big loaves of the *poilu* war bread and round boxes of the soft, evil-smelling cheese under one of its seats.

There was a general scramble for seats, and some of the other fellows immediately fell into an audible final snooze, while others "snitched" a bit of bread and cheese. It looked uninviting and nauseating at that hour, but by this time I had conquered my squeamishness and joined the latter group.

WELLMAN, INSTRUCTORS AND MECHANICS

It was some time before our conveyance actually got under way; but we were off at length, moving slowly past the low, dingy barracks, while the faint morning breeze, blowing over them, bore evidence to the fact that the sanitation there was of the most primitive order. Through the gray dawn and over a roadway, in which the ruts outnumbered the smooth spots, we jolted away; but it was better than walking. There was a little low laughter and jesting, but not a murmur of complaint—it was all part of the game. "*C'est la guerre*," as the French would have put it.

Arriving, I went to my machine—a real *air*-plane at last—as soon as it was assigned to me, and, with impatient eagerness to be off, listened while the monitor carefully showed me how the control stick worked,—I knew all about it already from watching and talking with others, *I thought*.

I listened impatiently while he gave me my final instructions about getting off the ground and landing, for my first trip, in fact all my flying in this third class, was to be devoted to the practice of these two things, and keeping a straight line in the air.

The usual preliminaries of starting were over at length, and, with my propeller a misty white circle before me, I started to taxi over the bubbly field in order to acquire the speed needed for the "take off"— some forty miles an hour. When I was certain that I had momentum enough,—I probably had had it seconds earlier,—I clinched my teeth, gave a mental "one, two, three, *go*," pulled back on my control stick— and went.

My first sensation was one of surprise at the sudden smoothness with which the machine under me was travelling; a mad ecstasy, over the thought that I was actually flying, succeeded it, and I gave a soundless whoop of joy, and looked down to see how the earth appeared from the magnificent height of twenty-five feet, and rushing backward at some sixty miles an hour.

Many of Jules Verne's imaginings have more than come true, and I may live some day to fly twenty-five *miles* above the ground, but I solemnly affirm that it will not seem so high to me as did that absurdly low altitude of as many feet.

My heart took a sudden jump upward, and, with but one idea— that of getting *out* of the air and back to *terra firma*—I pushed my control sharply forward and headed toward the ground. I had, only a few minutes before, been told painstakingly just what procedure to follow when making a landing, how to dip—or *piqué*—down until almost to the field, and then *redress*, or pull on my lever and straighten the plane out parallel to the ground, and so settle like a bird. Of course I forgot all about doing it, in my delight at seeing my machine draw near the solid earth again, with the result that I crashed into the ground almost head on, and, for the first of several times, felt the frail wings and *fuselage* collapse beneath me.

Half dazed, but wholly happy to be still alive and still intact myself, I sat amid the wreckage until others, including my monitor, came running up to extricate me. Some were grinning heartlessly. He was scowling a little; but, instead of giving me the tongue lacing that I richly deserved, he merely said, in a businesslike tone of voice, "Take machine number three, Wellman."

I had been in the air a little less than two minutes, and, on my very first attempt, had proved the truth of the words spoken in jest—the oldest of all aviation "wheeze"—that it is not the flying, but the *alighting*, that is dangerous. Still, *I had flown*, and, mixed with my self-disgust and anger over having been such an idiot, were the germs of the aerial craze.

I went to my second machine at once and, in a few moments, had completed a second ride, this time without mishap.

To a man who *has* flown, free from earthly limitations, in the clean, cool air where clouds are born, and has had the mastery of the three known dimensions, and a speed greater than has even been achieved on the earth, the old familiar sensations and thrills seem mild and trivial. Today I was out in an automobile, and speeded it up to sixty miles an hour. We hit only the high spots, but how crude this method of conveyance, during which one hits anything at all, seemed to me. I found myself unconsciously and continually pulling back on the wheel, as I would have on my control stick, to lift the motorcar into the air.

But this is anticipating.

Rain fell steadily for four days, from the third to the sixth, and, with no Fourth of July celebration, no letters from home, nothing to do but engage in the indoor sports, which soon palled, and the dismal weather, I was quite as blue as ever I had been in my life.

Then, with the return of the sunshine and real flying, everything became rosy again. This class, during which I flew in more or less straight lines back and forth across the field at an altitude of a score of feet, extended over a fortnight more, and, before it ended for me, I was able to alight in the manner which I had envied in others, without the jarring bump of a too abrupt dive, or the "pancake" thump of a too-flat drop.

Thus the middle of July brought my promotion to a still higher powered *Blériot*, with instructions to make the *tour de piste*—or flight around the field—in it, at an altitude of five hundred metres. With this came the reward for all the hard and irksome work that had gone before, and, oh, the untrammelled joy of skimming through the air, and seeing the earth below in its geometric figures of greens and browns, and the men looking like little black ants.

This class was, of course, intended to teach the pupil-*pilote* how to make his turns in the air, and that is quite a different thing from making them on the ground.

You know what happens to an automobile that tries to turn sharply on a level stretch of road, while going at a high speed. The same thing is true of an airplane. A turn with rudder only results in going off into a "wing-slip," which is nothing more nor less than a sidewise fall, and, just in the manner that the corners of a race track are banked to tilt a racing machine, and counteract the tendency to shoot straight ahead, and so go over when the turn is made, the airman has to provide a bank of air for himself in order to make a turn in safety.

He does this by tilting the plane down, in the direction which the turn is to take, by means of the side *ailerons*, or—in the *Blériot*—by warping the wings, as I have explained before.

The pressure of the air against the plane which is elevated, as the rudder swings the machine around, forms the necessary "bank." It is rather a neat operation and requires good judgment, for a too-sudden turn, while flying at full speed, causes such a tremendous atmospheric pressure on the lightly constructed wing that it is likely to collapse.

The doing of this, like everything else in flying, becomes second nature with practice, and demands no more thought than balancing a bicycle, but the beginner has to keep himself on the *qui vive*, and the nervous and physical strain that results is decidedly exhausting—at least I found it so.

On the morning of August the second I was, for the first time, two solid hours in the air, and, when I finally descended, I was almost "all in," and fairly trembling all over, not to mention being filthy, for the *Blériots* spit oil and grime frightfully and, after a long trip, we often looked like stokers.

During all this training in the air the monitors stayed on the ground and kept close enough watch on our doings to make mental notes of our mistakes and weaknesses, but I found them very patient and considerate in pointing them out and correcting them.

We Americans stood on a somewhat different plane from the ordinary French soldiers, for we were volunteers, come to aid them in their hour of need, and they appreciated that fact. Moreover, the discipline in the aviation was in nowise commensurate with that in other branches of the service; but there had to be a certain amount of it, nevertheless. One incident, in which it had a part, occurred about this time, and, although it was not a thing for the performers to boast of, it was amusing enough to be recounted.

Several of the American "colony" had kept their natural exuberance of spirits in as long as possible, and one evening went to the "corners"—as New Englanders might name the cluster of stores at the Avord depot—and proceeded to paint them red. Next morning they were all late to classes, and were promptly punished by imprisonment in the rude barrack jail, filling it to overflowing. Their term was to be three days in durance vile,—and vile it was; but that very night the Annamedes got into one of their free-for-all fights with knives, and the Yanks had to be released to make room for the new batch of prisoners. They were never called upon to finish their term.

Throughout the period of my earlier training we had heard persistent reports that Uncle Sam was about to take over the Lafayette Flying Corps, and my letters home were full of the good news, for it would mean flying under the Stars and Stripes, a thought which supplied an added incentive to the work. It did not happen while I was in the game, and, although I was to have the satisfaction of one day flying *over* Old Glory, it was to be under the tricolour of France.

To counteract this inspiring report, came an official order that all student *pilotes* at Avord should receive training in the heavy two-place bombing *Caudron* biplanes This spelled further delay in getting into the real action, and on top of that occurred several days of rain, and, although I knew that the fourth class, with its more interesting acrobatics was just ahead of me, I had another spell of the blues.

In looking back, the discomforts of my months at Avord seem trivial; but, with the heat, bugs, flies and especially bad weather, they seemed real enough when going through them.

CHAPTER 5

An "Upperclassman"

The third week in August was devoted to the *tour de piste* and the simpler acrobatics—an *à droit, à gauche,* a *serpentine* and three *spirales*—performed in a still more powerful *Blériot,* which had an eighty horse-power rotative Gnome motor. With this class the real "thrills" began. I was much too elated and excited to be frightened; but, when a beginner makes his first dives in corkscrew curves from a height of thirty-five hundred feet, with the motor cut off and nothing solid under him except a monoplane, which is a rather ticklish craft to manage, especially when the air is rough, he is pretty certain to get some sensations which he never had before.

The *à droit* is simple—when you know how! It merely consists of *piquéing* down with the motor off, then, as you approach the earth, you bank sharply, and make a right hand turn and instantly straighten your machine out either to make a landing, or continue your flight. Of course the *à gauche* is a similar turn by the left flank.

The *serpentine* explains itself, and a *spirale* is a joyslide to a point directly below the one from which you start, on an invisible spiral staircase with the plane tilted all the time. It beats the most ex- citing roller coaster all hollow, and, since there are no rails to guide your machine, the novice has to keep his wits about him, for, if he *piqués* too sharply, off he goes into a spinning nose dive.

After the first attempt, during which my throat felt a bit con-stricted, and my heart beat an unrhythmical tattoo against my ribs, I began to enjoy those headlong rushes toward earth, and the sudden straightening out of the machine, by tilting its elevator up at exactly the right moment.

When I had satisfied the monitor that I had mastered this style of air travel, I was given two days' leave before starting in with the

Caudron.

The school had narrowed down materially by this time, as many of the newer comers had been shipped to another one—for we had not planes enough to take care of them—and others had failed, or had been discharged because of illness. I felt that I was safe now, however, having made what the *capitaine* termed very creditable progress. I must have had the constitution of a horse, for I had stood up under the strenuous work and the terrible food, and had not missed a single morning or afternoon session of flying.

My forty-eight-hour stay in Paris began on August nineteenth, and it proved to be all that I had anticipated.

For the first time in my life I experienced the real delight of being utterly lazy, of lounging around in a comfortable hotel chair and of sleeping between linen sheets.

I also made the acquaintance, by means of a letter of introduction from an American girl who was a mutual friend, of the delightful woman who was to be my war godmother, Miss Grace Wood. She was middle aged, big-hearted—in fact one of the noblest women it has ever been my good fortune to meet—and an indefatigable worker in the *Croix Rouge* of Paris. From that date on, she was to care for me like a second mother.

Paris looked decidedly different than it had when I left it, nearly three months previous, for now I found Yankee soldiers and sailors on the streets in numbers, and how I "chinned" with them, getting all the latest news from home, down to the dry-as-dust batting and fielding averages in the baseball leagues! Mine was a real rest, and, when I took the train back toward Avord, I had to drive myself with all my will power to face the opposite conditions to which I knew I was returning. However, the "call of the air" was more insistent than ever, and it increased to the point of madness as a full fortnight passed without bringing a single day with conditions fit for flying.

During this spell the newly established Y. M. C. A. club, in a small room in one of the barracks, proved another God-send. All kinds of sandwiches, chocolate, soap and other little luxuries were sold at the lowest possible prices, and, last but by no means least, real *American cigarettes.* You cannot know what that meant to us unless you have smoked the cheap French kinds, without wearing a gas mask. Then the room had the usual equipment for reading, writing and amusements, including "canned" music of the "Made in America" brand—it was, in fact, a little bit of the good old U. S. A., in the heart of France.

It would be impossible to overestimate the good work being done by that, and similar institutions, at and near the front.

I had fully expected to start training in the new type of machine immediately upon my return to the school, but none was ready for me. Every available *Caudron* had been smashed by the Russian students, who were wonderfully bad aviators—fearless, but sadly lacking in air sense.

For nearly two more weeks, after the weather cleared again, I continued my practice work in a *Blériot*, one day establishing a very fair altitude record for a pupil in a monoplane—thirty-five hundred metres. More than once I kept up my afternoon session for five hours, at the end of it being too dog-tired to return to the barracks, and, instead, stretched myself out on the bare ground beneath one of the hangars and slept there, fully dressed.

These continued postponements of my final work at Avord, and the achievement of the coveted "brevet" which was to crown it, were disheartening; but, as a matter of fact, did no harm, for one who is learning to be a fighting *pilote* cannot imbibe too much experience in the fundamentals. Nevertheless, it was difficult to be philosophical then, for the thought of the possibility of having to spend any part of the Winter there was unendurable, and I used to get indigo blue at times, which was not difficult, for I was generally tired to death at night. I drew some slight selfish comfort from the knowledge that I was, after all, faring better than several of my acquaintances, for a few had been obliged to leave the school and others reduced from the one-place machines to those of the bombing type, which sealed their doom as far as ever driving a fighting *chasse* plane at the front was concerned. This was a thing that we all dreaded.

My first injury—a minor one—came early in September. One morning, while I was cranking my own machine by spinning the propeller, it kicked like an army mule and rather badly strained my back, picking out a spot which had been hurt in football some years before. The injury did not lay me up, but it proved rather painful and—worse—knocked out my digestion for the first time. The gentle diet of horsemeat, lentils and French war-bread is not the best thing in the world for a weakened stomach,

September fourteenth stood out as a Red Letter Day, for it not only brought my biplane, but several long-delayed boxes from home, containing flannels, a wonderful sweater, candy and cigarettes. I felt like a millionaire. The heavier underwear was most welcome at that time, for, with the coming of Fall, and flying at higher altitudes, I was beginning to suffer from the cold. It is astonishing how much keener the air is when one gets a few hundred feet above the ground. It has a bite all its own.

The shift to a biplane was a welcomed one, and the new machine surprised me with its steadiness. It was like leaving a rowboat that is tossed about by the smallest waves, and boarding an ocean liner. Still the controls were much "harsher," and required the exercise of almost double the strength required in a *Blériot*.

The week ushered in by Sunday, the sixteenth, was one of many incidents. First came the news from the acrobatic school at Pau that William Meeker, a lad who for some weeks had been one of my closest chums, although he was a bit ahead of me in training, had been killed. Capitaine Terrio had pronounced him a wonderful *pilote*, when he graduated from our school, but the "luck" had not been with him. His motor had stopped when he was only a little above the ground, his machine had gone into a wing-slip when he banked a bit too hard, and he had crashed down to death. This report confirmed me in my belief that, in training at least, *better be safe than sorry*, is the motto to follow.

This may surprise such of my personal acquaintances as read this; but it is a fact that I followed it pretty consistently during my early work, and recommend it to all beginners in aviation. Later, when you have gained the mastery of your machine, you can take chances—and I did, a-plenty.

The very next evening I witnessed a piece of the other kind of luck, coupled with some wonderful flying. One of our monitors, who was also a French Ace, got caught in a sudden and violent tempest, with lightning, a gale of wind and rain. We stood below and watched his machine as the sharp flashes of lightning illuminated it against the rolling black clouds, and it was being tossed about unmercifully. Only a miracle could save him, it seemed, but by a transcendent display of coolness and marvellous control he brought his machine safe to earth and made a perfect landing, thereby escaping what looked to us like certain death. I have never seen such a thrilling exhibition as the way he handled that tiny, frail aircraft in the heart of the storm.

On September nineteenth the school was visited by several United States officers who came to examine us for immediate admission to Uncle Sam's service, not as a unit, however, but as individuals. Their tests were extremely simple, or we had been so well trained that they seemed so to me, and I passed them easily. Yet, when the time came when I might have taken the oath and become an American airman, I ducked it. This may seem strange to you, for, as I have said, I had been crazy to make that very shift, and I knew, moreover, that, upon obtaining my brevet, I would almost certainly get a second lieutenancy with pay of two hundred dollars a month, against the six that I was then getting from the French government, and the *eleven* to which I was looking forward. To be perfectly frank, the consideration of additional compensation carried a strong appeal, for the minimum expenses and an occasional real "feed," ate up my monthly allowance in no time.

The reason that I did not change over then, was because I realized that I would be wholly subject to American orders, and the word went around that in all probability those who did change would not be allowed to remain and complete their training at Avord and Pau. Despite the hardships, the schooling there was the best obtainable then, and I determined to stick and round mine out. I felt that if I could really become an "A-1" *pilote*—whether my title was that of American Lieutenant or French Corporal—I would be of more value to the Allies, and so to my own country in the long run, especially if to my schooling I could add a period of actual flying and fighting with the old-timers at the front. There was always the possibility of shifting later.

Finally, what America might be able to do in the "air-line," for some time to come, was problematical, and I did not want to take the chance of waiting, perhaps for months. I wanted to fly and *fight* at the first possible moment.

Thus the chance that I had wanted, came, and I put it resolutely behind me. I resumed my work with the heavy *Caudron* under the instruction of Lieutenant de Kurnier and on Friday, the twenty-seventh of September, had the great satisfaction of being told that in the afternoon I should try the first of the three final tests, which, if met successfully, would give me my brevet. It went by the name of the *petit voyage*, and in my case meant a fifty-mile trip 'cross country from Avord to Chateauroux, and return.

At the hour set for the start of my first journey away from the home fold, there was a pretty stiff head-wind blowing; but I got off, lifted my slow, cumbersome but reliable craft to an altitude of seventy-five hundred feet, and set sail. Like all other ships bound for foreign ports, whether on the sea or in the air, mine was equipped with map and compass, and in addition had a gasoline gauge, an altimeter, to indicate the height from the ground, and a dial registering the number of the motor's revolutions per minute.

From a mile and a half in the air the country beneath appeared like a different world from that which I had been accustomed to, for it stretched flatly away for immense distances in every direction; familiar objects lost their distinctive features and took on geometric shapes; fields and little forests became patchwork squares of subdued and varying colours, like an old-fashioned and oft-washed quilt spread over some sleeping giant; houses were mere toy things like those of a Japanese table decoration; roads were coarse white thread; haystacks white pinheads, and little lakes, bright new silver dollars.

As my machine undulated, the whole world seemed to rock gently back and forth.

Even my steady craft was tossed about considerably by the air waves, and, since my progress was like that of a boat bucking a strong head-tide, it took me a full hour to make my port of destination. On the earth, fifty miles in sixty minutes is going some, but in the air it is barely crawling. There are no fixed objects to flash past.

When almost over the aviation field outside the little gray town of Chateauroux—located by means of my topographical map—I *piquéd* down and made a successful landing. Then, after getting my tank re-filled with *essence*, as the French call gasoline, and having my paper signed by the commandant of the field, I started for home, sailing before the wind.

Half the distance had been covered when my magneto went sud-denly bad, and I experienced the unpleasant sensation of having my motor stop short, which left me with no motive power and more than a mile in the air. It sounds desperate, but in reality the danger in such a case increases in adverse ratio to the distance from the ground. Just as a sailor likes to have plenty of "sea-room" in a storm, an aviator likes to have plenty of "air-room." Nevertheless, it certainly gave me a series of thrills and a rather empty feeling inside as I volplaned earthward by easy degrees, coasting down the gentle slope of an airy mountainside. Again it was a case of the danger being in the "landing," and I had plenty of worry, for I did not know whether I should have the good luck to strike a cleared field, or the bad luck to plump into a wood or through a farmhouse roof. As the land rose rapidly I saw what I sought, a field, and made for it, landing without accident.

It took me only a little time to find and fix the trouble in my magneto; but, before I was ready to reascend, quite a crowd of open-mouthed peasants, in their quaint costumes, had gathered, and, when I went up, it was with their names and initials pencilled all over my fuselage, and with several bunches of field flowers, gifts of my brief acquaintances. I quite looked the part of a hero.

Dusk had fallen before my flight ended safely at home, and that night I turned in with the feeling that I had really taken a step forward on the road to the front.

The day following was the most strenuous of my whole training career at Avord. After nine hours of almost consecutive flying I came to earth so weary that I could scarcely totter; but proud, and too happy for words, since I knew that I had finished my appointed tasks and earned my brevet.

That morning I had repeated the *petit voyage* of the day before without incident, although, going out, my engine laboured like an old horse with the heaves. Then I did my first *grand voyage*. This meant a trip to Chateauroux, fifty miles; thence one to another small town named Romorantin forty-eight miles; and back home to Avord, fifty miles, getting my paper signed at each place visited. Nothing of special interest distinguished this triangular voyage, and, late in the afternoon, I started to cover the trail again, the other way around.

On the last leg of it, when dusk was already falling like a soft mantle over the earth below, a sudden storm blew up, and I plunged into a flock of billowy gray clouds. They blinded and seemed almost to stifle me. For a quarter of an hour I wove in and out through them, half the time being unable to see my hand on the control stick, now coming out above them into the evening sunlight, which tinged their rolling upper surfaces with a golden glow, and then below, so that they formed a soft, dark canopy just over my head. Tired of this at last, I *piquéd* down from my then altitude of twenty-five hundred metres to one of five hundred, where the flying was clearer, but very rough, and when I reached home it was with a sigh of hearty thanksgiving that I struck *terra firma*, and received the congratulations of my friends.

On Saturday, September twenty-ninth, I received my brevet and *pilote's* license—a gold and silver wreath with two wings—with a brief word of commendation from the commandant. The exultant satisfaction that it brought with it more than repaid me for all the petty discomforts of the camp. I was now a corporal in the French army and entitled to wear a single golden wing on either side of my collar. They somehow seemed to me to carry magic, like those on Mercury's staff,

RÉPUBLIQUE FRANÇAISE

MINISTÈRE DE LA GUERRE

Aéronautique Militaire

BREVET
D'AVIATEUR MILITAIRE

Le Ministre de la Guerre,

Vu l'Instruction en date du ... 1912 sur la délivrance du Brevet relatif à la conduite des appareils d'aviation

Vu l'avis favorable des Commissions d'examen des candidats au dit Brevet

Décerne à la date du **29 Septembre 1917**
à M. **Wellman William**
Soldat
le Brevet d'Aviateur Militaire

Fait à Paris, le ...

P.O. Le Chef de ...

9.045

MR. WELLMAN'S COMMISSION AS AVIATOR
IN THE FRENCH ARMY

Furthermore, I was entitled to ten days' leave, but this time the privilege was only an irritation, as I did not have money enough even to buy a ticket to Paris—and, of course, "leave" without "Paris" was no leave at all.

The front now began to seem mighty close ahead; but it was separated from me by a final brief training at Avord in a *Nieuport*—the light, fast, fighting machine commonly used at the front—and the advanced acrobatics at Pau and Plessis Belleville.

Said quickly, it did not seem like much; but once again I was doomed to spend two solid weeks in twiddling my thumbs and seeing everything through dark blue glasses, for the weather was awful. Rain, high winds and mists were on the program day after day, so that I succeeded in adding scarcely anything to my record of fifty hours' flying. Fifty hours, three thousand minutes—at a dollar a minute, three thousand dollars! That is what a private teacher would have charged at home, and I had got it for nothing!

By this time the conditions of living had begun to get on my nerves, and my unhappiness was further increased by the fact that the French-American flying corps had been broken up by the departure of a considerable number of my former comrades, who had joined the U. S. service. During this time, too, our barracks were shifted to an old barn, but recently vacated by a number of horses, and even the fresh coat of whitewash could not successfully disguise that fact. You American boys, in your new model camps, will never know the "horrors of war" as illustrated by the best that stricken France could do for her men in training. But, on looking back at my experiences, I am not sure but that mine was the better part, for it made the front seem like heaven by comparison. You have got to reverse the procedure.

Even in writing this I feel in a hurry to get away from Avord for good, so I will not pause to describe the wonderful little *Nieuports* until later.

Eventually we got a few fairly respectable days and, to my equal delight and surprise, I was "graduated" on October twenty-first. I had gone through the school in five months, outstripping several who had preceded me there.

During this brief preliminary training in a *Nieuport* I made my first acquaintance with the "Vickers" rapid fire gun—which I was later to use—taking it apart and studying the construction. As I was not deeply versed in mechanical lore, this gun on an airplane impressed me as something uncanny, for it sent seven hundred shots a minute *through* the whirling blades of the propeller, which, in a fast-flying *chasse* machine, revolve no less than seventeen hundred times every sixty seconds. Think of the delicate mechanism required to time the two accurately. I have since read in the newspaper that the explanation of this seeming impossibility is that the shafts of the propeller blades are sheathed with metal at the point near the axis where the bullets pass, and that approximately thirty *per cent*, of them *do* hit. That certainly is absolutely untrue in the case of any machine I ever used or saw. The blades were all of unprotected wood, and occasionally a shot would pierce them clean, the reason being, I was told, that the gun had become overheated, and exploded a cartridge out of its proper timing.

Two incidents, not on the calendar, happened just before I left the school. First, one of the wheels of my machine came off as I was about to leave the ground on a practice flight, and both plane and I turned two complete somersaults without serious damage to either. Then, one afternoon, while I was cranking my machine, I foolishly allowed my head to get too near the spinning propeller, and received an uppercut on my right cheek, just below the eye, the blow neatly slicing off a piece of skin. It was a close shave in two senses, and my fortunate escape from a more serious injury reminded some of the old-timers that, early in the Spring, a young Yankee student had actually been decapitated in that manner.

I shook the dust of Avord from my feet with no regrets, although I left many good friends there, and, on the twenty-first of October, in company with David Judd, went to Paris for forty-eight hours before having to report at Pau. By this time my apparently slight head wound had begun to suppurate, and it looked so bad, and felt so painful, that one of the first things I did upon reaching the French metropolis was to visit Dr. Gros. The cut was too close to my eye to take any chances with, I felt.

He found that the cheek bone had been splintered and that a sliver of it was still in the wound. A slight operation was necessary to remove it, and I left his office looking like a real hero, with my uniform and bandaged head and eye. One musical show was the extent of my frivolities in Paris that trip; but I played the part of a glutton when it came to eating, sleeping and "lazing."

On the twenty-fourth Judd and I left Southward, bound for the last stage of the long journey toward the goal of my desires—"The Fighting Front."

CHAPTER 6

"Stunts"

Pau, a famous summer resort of some thirty-five thousand inhabitants—peace basis,—located in the extreme south of France, with Spain but a few miles distant across the snow-peaked Pyrenees, is wonderfully beautiful. After Avord it was like Paradise to me.

I hope someday to visit again the lovely city, with its magnificent hotels and merry recreations, for, although our camp was some little distance away, and the weather was turning cold, so that I was there only two weeks, chocked full of work, the place is one of wholly delightful memories.

"Duke" Sinclair, Judd and I were still together—three modern musketeers,—and our quarters overlooked the beautiful rolling fields that stretched away, bisected by a pleasant, winding stream, to the foot of the mountain steeps. Never before had I seen such glorious sunsets and sunrises, with the glowing multi-coloured tints reflected on the glistening mountain tops, and, since the old schedule of working from sunup to sundown held, I never missed one of them.

Pau was our "finishing school." We were done with the drudgery of the "reading, 'riting and 'rithmetic" of aviation, and ready to learn the airy graces without which both a society *débutante* and a flying fighter are helpless.

The machines used here were the real fighting *Nieuports* of varying sizes and speeds. What a beauty I thought the first one that was given me to fly, a slender little thoroughbred compared with the dray-horse *Caudron.* Its *fuselage* was long and tapering, its wings only eighteen metres from tip to tip and its engine and eighty horse-power rotary Rhone, which alone was worth something over twenty-five hundred dollars. Yet even this was low-powered and cumbersome beside the type I was soon to fly. Nevertheless, it could make better than a hundred miles an hour, and the exhilaration produced by travelling through the stinging cold air at that speed was the most glorious sensation I had ever known. When it came to making a landing at a speed scarcely less, it took a perfect eye and a no less perfect judgment, not to mention nerve.

The first class in "stunts" was called the *vol de groupe*. In plain English it was a game of follow the leader. One man would set the pace and the other, for we worked in pairs at first and later in quartets, would follow fifty metres behind and the same distance above—-if he could.

The first day I went up trailing "Juddy," and at first I flew so close that I could read the small letter on his *essence* tank. He pointed upward in a steep spiral climb and in five minutes we had reached an altitude of two thousand metres—more than a mile. How those *Nieuports* could climb!

For two hours he circled about, with me following as closely as possible to the prescribed distance. With one's machine going at a hundred miles an hour, you can perhaps imagine how hard it is to keep at anything like a stated distance, especially as you have no idea what the "leader" is going to do next. Judd might *piqué* suddenly and leave me shooting off into space like a rifle ball, and I could imagine him laughing at me. It was a great game, and, although it was physically tiring, I was sorry to see him head for the field.

We flew almost every possible moment during the second, third and fourth of November in this *vol de groupe*. The last flight alternated between three thousand, and fifty metre altitudes, and, at the lower level, it was as exciting as any steeple chase. This time Sinclair was leader, and three wild boys never played more foolish pranks than he, Judd and I that afternoon. To end up, he spotted a train, and led us in circles around and only a little above it, like dolphins playing about a slow tramp steamer. If our motors had quit when we were at that small altitude it would have spelt the end of all games, but luck was with us, and we certainly gave the passengers a few thrills not called for by their tickets.

The next day I was moved up a rung on the ladder leading to success, and given, to use in my tracking, a hundred and ten horsepowered, thirteen metre winged plane, still a *Nieuport*, whose speed was one hundred and thirty miles an hour. This was the most powerful and nimble plane I had ever flown, and the feeling of having mastery over it was delicious, for it answered to the slightest touch.

There followed a few days of individual practice in the more complicated "stunts," without the knowledge of which a fighting pilot would be helpless against an expert adversary. They may be said to correspond to the "foot-work" of a skilled boxer.

The simplest was the loop the loop, which needs no description. Then followed the *vrille*, or spinning nose dive, with motor cut off, and this, too, is almost self-explanatory. Of course the plane dives vertically and at the same time turns on its own axis. I was later to learn that a great variety of accidents would throw my plane into the *vrille*, and, in order to enter it deliberately, it was only necessary to *piqué* vertically down by dipping my rear controls and then tip the side *ailerons* either way, whereupon the machine would proceed to imitate a Looping the Loop magnified corkscrew in an airy bottle containing a draught as exhilarating as champagne, and almost as "heady "at times, for the sudden dive from the rarer atmosphere of the high altitudes to the denser air near the earth produced a pressure which I sometimes had to counteract by compressing the air inside my head with cheeks extended.

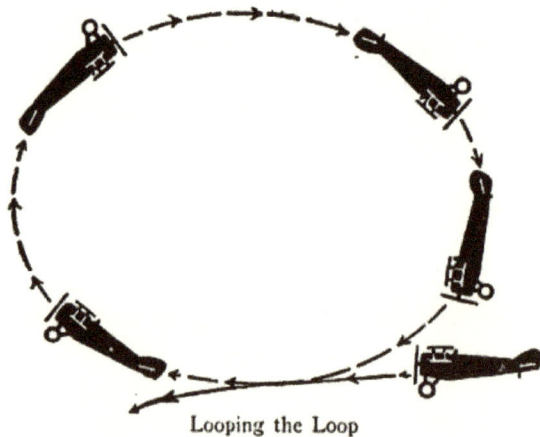

Looping the Loop

Here let me answer a question which has been asked me often—"What do you aviators wear to protect your eyes and faces from the rush of wind?"The answer is, "Nothing." A leather helmet, fur-lined, covers the head like a child's knitted woollen one; but the only protection that the face gets is that furnished by a glass windshield like that on an automobile. "But," sometimes say my questioners, "isn't a glass shield dangerous? Suppose it is shattered by a bullet."The answer is, if that happens the chances are nine hundred and ninety-nine out of a thousand that the flyer will not be worrying about flying glass, or anything else for long. Of course, some airmen wear goggles, but I never did.

Then followed the *tournant*. It proved to be very simple and amusing. You merely give the control stick a swift jerk to one side and back, and the plane rolls completely over in the air as quick as a wink. Its particular purpose is to make your machine a more difficult object to hit when you are being shot at.

I next tackled "Russian Mountain," the *renversement* and the vertical *virage*, and since they are all highly important to the fighter and I shall have occasion to use the terms frequently hereafter, I will endeavour to make their meaning clear, both by word and picture description.

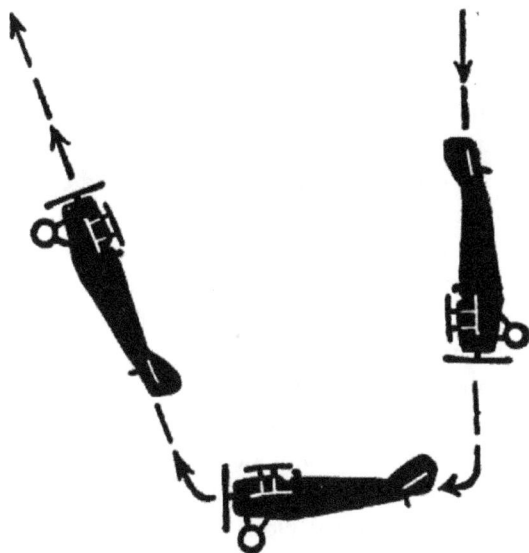

A " Russian Mountain "

The first mentioned consists merely in diving with motor going, then shutting it off so that the strain on the plane will not be more than it can stand up under, and suddenly straightening out parallel to the earth by pushing the control stick from you and so elevating the rear *ailerons*, then starting the motor and again raising the elevator, which causes your plane to shoot upward. The machine is not the only thing to feel the strain of these abrupt checks and turns in midair. You who have ridden on a steep roller-coaster with sharp dips, can guess what I mean, and, if you can imagine the speed increased twofold, you will understand how it came about that I was minus my breakfast after the first time that I tried it.

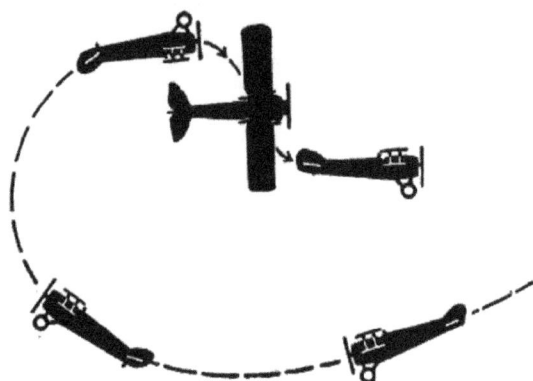

A *Renversement*

The second, the *renversement*, changes the direction of your plane in the following manner: You start upward in a loop the loop, and, when flying head downward, cut off the motor and by tilting the side *ailerons* go into a wing-slip and continue this in a semicircle until your machine has turned over and resumed a horizontal position going in the direction opposite from the one in which it was headed a few seconds before. This is a highly useful trick when an enemy is behind and above you, and you want to reverse positions so as to dive on *him*. Flying upside down sounds desperate, I suppose; but it is not. You are held in, both by centrifical force and the body straps which come up under your thighs, cross your shoulders and fasten over your stomach by a mechanical device which will instantly spring open and release you upon being struck a smart blow. Besides, most of these tricks are pulled off so quickly that you have no time to consider the fact that you are not in the position normal to man, and, when you are two or three miles in the air, the earth has ceased to be the thing by which you govern your movements.

The vertical *virage* is a quick reversal of direction, made by turning sharply on the same plane, with your machine banked until it is tilted almost at right angles to the earth.

A Vertical *Virage*

62

I went through the whole performance, loops, *vrilles, tournants, virages*, and *renversements*, in a single day, but it was no unusual thing for a chap to be so sick at first that he would be laid up for two or three days. This happened in Sinclair's case.

Then I tackled the so-called *vol de précision*, which was another game—a game of quoits, with your machine as the quoit. A small white circle, some twenty yards in diameter, was painted upon the middle of the field, and we were told to go up to an altitude of a thousand metres, cut our motors, plane until the propeller was motionless and then *piqué* and head for the circle. Landing within it twice in succession passed us out of this class. I accomplished it after one failure; but Tom Hitchcock, who arrived at Pau soon after I did, was successful on his first two attempts and, in fact, went through the school there as he had at Avord, "a-flying." This test, of course, was one of eyesight in aiming for the mark and of judgement in *redressing*, or pulling up at exactly the right moment. The machine hit the ground like a bat out of hell.

The final class was termed the *vol de combat*, and, although it was still only a game, it fired my blood and made me wild to try out the real thing. The first half represented an actual fight over the first line trenches, whose location was marked by the little river below, and it was patterned as closely as possible upon what we were later to experience almost daily in dead earnest.

Three of the expert French flyers, with a leader, were detailed to represent the Boche, and the rest of the class, some ten in number, with a veteran in command, were the Allies. We went up as opposing patrols, putting into practice what we had learned in the *vol de groupe*, and, for some minutes, flew back and forth on opposite sides of the stream. At last their leader gave the signal to attack by moving his *manche à balai* rapidly from side to side which made his plane rock violently, his idea being to catch us unaware and break up our group. The "enemy" obeyed, and sprang to the attack.

On the hood directly in front of me was my "gun"—a perfect imitation of a Vickers, fixed and pointed forward through the propeller; but, instead of a belt of death-dealing cartridges with which to annihilate the Boche, it contained a camera and film. The shutter was operated by pulling a regulation trigger attached to my control stick, and just below the little wheel that topped it. The trigger was pulled by the left hand, of course.

We had previously received instruction on the various methods of attacking an enemy—the theory of assaulting a monoplane like our own being to gain altitude on it, and dive, from the rear if possible, for, as its gun was "fixed" and pointing forward like our own, the pilot could shoot only by aiming his whole machine at us. I selected my "victim" from the oncoming enemy planes, gained my altitude over him, and, with the joy of battle—even if it were only a sham—sending the blood singing in my ears, I swooped down at him, and "shot."

The combat was over in a few moments, and I returned to earth to seek out my late opponent and tell him, gloatingly, that he was theoretically dead. My triumph was short lived. When the film from my gun was developed it showed a beautiful expanse of clear sky. Of course, to have registered a kill, the hostile plane would have had to appear on it.

I may as well state here that in actual battle the range is usually obtained by firing flaming, or "tracer," bullets, whose course is visible in the form of a small streak of fire and smoke. Moreover, since machines travelling at a hundred and twenty miles and upward, pass each other with terrific speed and offer a most illusive target, the custom is never to open fire until you are almost on top of the enemy. Twenty-five yards is too far for accuracy; fifteen is more certain.

The last half of this battle training took the form of an attack on a Boche bombing plane. In a small pond there was constructed a canvas target, the shape and size of a big "*Gotha*," its actual prototype being a huge unwieldy three-place plane with triple motors and propeller.

I was instructed to ascend and do a few warming-up acrobatic stunts, and then finish by doing a *virage*, starting at only five hundred metres above the ground. Just before making the horizontal turn I was to let the enemy have it. For this I had, of course, a real Vickers gun, which would continue to shoot as long as my finger remained on the trigger, at least it would until the belt of cartridges was exhausted, or it jammed.

It did very well for a practice performance; but it was not a real test of such fighting, because, in the first place, at such a low altitude you had to pay too much attention to your plane to give a great deal to your marksmanship, and, in the second, no self-respecting pilot attacks a two or more place machine from above. The observer or bomber in the rear seat is also a gunner, and *his* weapon is swivelled, so that you furnish him an easy mark if you dive down at him.

On my first attempt I landed ten out of a possible hundred shots in the target, and on my second bettered this by two, which, the instructor said, was not bad shooting. Nor was it, considering the fact that we had had no gunnery practice, and the aiming had to be done, not with the gun but with the machine. *One* shot in a vital spot would do the business!

My fortnight at Pau was one of unalloyed delight, and its successful termination brought my commission as corporal, and a certificate upon which the commandant wrote the words, " A born aviator, but crazy." (I told you that I took chances, *after* I had learned the rudiments.) In fact the common expression among French flyers was, "*Tous les Americains sont fous*"—which, being interpreted, means, "All the Americans are crazy," and it was a term complimentary rather than otherwise.

Moreover, this ended my worries, for, with my certificate, went a recommendation that I be given a *Spad* monoplane fighting *chasse* (the word "Spad" being coined from the initials of the makers) which was the fastest French plane then used, having a two hundred and twenty horse-power fixed Espano-Suiza motor.

I was sent immediately, on November twelfth, to Plessis Belleville to await my assignment to an *escadrille* at the front, and, with an occasional brief leave spent in Paris, remained there until December third.

Plessis Belleville, a few hours' ride outside the Metropolis, somehow sounded delightful, as though it might be a charming little suburb. It was in reality a good deal of a dump, and, since the barracks were then overcrowded and the army canteen had been closed for some reason or other, I had to hire a room in an inexpensive but clean lodging house, run by an energetic gray-haired little English woman named Mrs. Abbott, and buy my own meals.

If money had been scarce before, now it seemed to vanish on wings, and only a belated gift from home, promptly sent in response to an earlier wail, saved me from committing crime. Moreover, I had only one uniform, and, since I would have had to go to bed to have this pressed, it went wrinkled, which was disconcerting, for my companions told me that the French government liked to have its men well dressed when they were captured by the Germans, and I did not like to face the thought of disgracing the flag under which I flew.

However, I hoped for the best, trusting that Santa Claus would prove to be a mind reader, and spent almost every moment of the much diminished daylight in training flights in my wonderful new machine, and in gun practice.

The first *Spad* which they gave me to try out in had a hundred and fifty horse-power, super-compressed engine, which developed one hundred and eighty. It mounted a single Vickers gun shooting through the propeller as I have described.

Plessis Belleville ended my postgraduate specializing course of training. It also very nearly ended my life. As I have said, I flew daily whenever the weather offered the slightest possibility of going up, even though it might be cloudy and windy, for by this time I had come to regard myself as a competent pilot, fully able to handle a plane under all ordinary conditions, and was at the same time determined to practice, practice, practice until I was more than merely competent.

Here let me say that mere wind of a velocity that ten years ago would have made flying suicidal, has now no terrors to the pilot of a modern, high-powered, speedy machine. We can ride an ordinary gale and laugh at it, although there is little laughing done when it comes to landing in one. The air is always more treacherous near the ground. Nor are the much talked of and dreaded "air-holes" of a decade ago any longer things of terror. They are present, of course, and occasionally your machine will drop suddenly in one; but the speedy planes generally slide over them as does a flying skater over a stretch of thin ice. Heavy mist and very low hanging clouds—in fact anything which produces what the sailors call "low visibility"—are the bane of the flyer's existence, for one cannot feel his way through the air as he does on the ground, and it is a bit difficult to avoid an unsuspected obstacle when coming suddenly upon it, at a speed of better than a hundred miles an hour.

On one of the last days of my work at Plessis Belleville the gray, wintry-looking clouds were very low and lowering, not more than three hundred yards above the earth, but I flew morning and afternoon, nevertheless, and about four o'clock was back on the field for a new supply of gas, when the monitor called out, "Last ride of the night," and then, turning to me, added, "Wellman, take your machine."

I obeyed, got started, and climbed in leisurely circles until my plane was just about to nose inquisitively into the unpleasant moist bank above, when I straightened out and glanced downward. I could not see a thing. The world had vanished, swallowed up in fog, dull white and impenetrable. Once, in the movies, I had seen a thrilling melodrama in which the floor of a secret chamber rose ceilingwards to crush the imprisoned heroine. I felt a good deal as though something of the sort was happening to me. Of course I could dive through *that* floor much as Alice went through the dissolving looking-glass, but in my case it would not help much if I could not see the earth until I felt it.

Still, there was nothing else to be done, and I turned to the left as is customary in making a *tour de piste*, *piquéd* down, and headed for the spot where I thought that I might be able to pick up the two railroad stations as guideposts in locating the field. You know the feeling of a small child lost in the dark. I had it. I did not have the faintest idea where to turn, or whether I was right side up, and it was steadily growing darker. Suddenly my motor determined my course of action for me by stopping dead, and then my sensations changed from helpless uncertainty to acute anxiety, for there was nothing left for me to do but dive from my altitude of two hundred and fifty metres, and trust to luck.

I braced my feet and gritted my teeth to keep my heart a part of my anatomy, while the cold sweat started out all over me. Suddenly the mist grew a little thinner, and I dimly made out the formation of a small field, heavily wooded on either side, not more than a hundred and fifty feet below. Without my motor to pull me clear, and lacking altitude to glide over the tree tops I could do nothing but keep on into the pocket. As I rushed downward I realized that I was headed into a field filled with old barbwire entanglements erected by the Boche when they were stopped at this place, during the first Battle of the Marne, in their drive for Paris in 1914.

Now my fright, growing out of my utter helplessness, turned to anger at Fate in playing me such a scurvy trick. With clinched teeth I put into practice the old rule, "when in doubt, keep on," and went into the wire like a football player hitting the line. My machine crashed to a sudden stop, I felt myself being shot from it like a rock out of a catapult, there was a blinding flash like lightning before my eyes, and then . . . nothing.

My next impression was produced by the taste of some vile French wine. My head began to split open with pain, and I dazedly unclosed my eyes to the sight of the sides of a rude farm wagon. I was still alive, then, I thought with some astonishment, and I found myself dumbling whispering the words, "*Laugh and Live*, God bless old Douglas Fairbanks." The cheery philosophy contained in his book, which had been my only literature for months, had come to my aid.

What had happened during my absence from the world of conscious things, was this, I found. My fall into the wire and solo flight through the air, which had ended in a headfirst dive into the ground, had been witnessed by a farmer's lad. He had taken it for granted that I was dead, and had hurried to town, half an hour's trip distant, to get his father. The latter had returned with his farm horse and wagon and found me, an hour after my accident, lying unconscious, and with my face ground into the dirt. Naturally my machine was smashed to bits, but, by the grace of God, I was merely bunged up a little, and, although I was kept in the camp hospital for three days, at the end of the period I came out as good as new.

On Saturday, December the first, I was given my fur-lined combination flying suit, warm boots and duffle bag to keep them in, signed out of the school, and told to go to Paris and await my final assignment to the front. Moreover, the same day brought a big package of heavy underwear, socks and a sweater from home, and a marvellous comfort bag from another source, so I was fully equipped for the fray.

CHAPTER 7

Boche Bombs

My schooling was ended. I was a full-fledged birdman, and, eager to try my wings in the work for which they had been trained, I went to Paris.

A whole weekend was mine before I had to report for duty with *Escadrille* N. 87 in the Lorraine sector near Nancy—my orders having reached me the same day that I reached Paris—and I resolved to make the most of it.

To my great pleasure one of the first persons whom I met at the hotel *François Choiseul* on Rue Saint Honoré was a charming and courageous American girl, whom I knew very well. That evening we went together to see a musical comedy, which I enjoyed almost as much as though I had been able to understand the words. After all, anyone who has attended such in America knows that the lines are non-essential, and this is doubly true in Paris.

On our way back to the hotel we stopped for light refreshments at the *Café de la Paix*. It was nearly midnight when we stepped from its brilliant lights into the cold, clear night. The streets were quiet, few pedestrians were about, and, high above, the night sky seemed inestimably distant, and the stars merely sparkles of diamond dust.

Night air raids by the Boche barbarians had become so frequent an occurrence that it seemed almost strange not to hear the air-splitting clamour of the *Alerte*, and the sounds of explosions, nearby and deafening, or rumbling in the distance.

With little conversation we walked together under the spell of the peaceful night. One instant the silence was that of a slumbering city. The next it was shattered by the most appalling detonation and crash. The earth shuddered and the rush of air from the concussion nearly threw us from our feet.

Before the reverberations of the first explosion had ceased there came another, but a little farther off, and instantly a third. Then, to the terrible clatter of falling buildings and the terrified cries from the few people on the streets and from windows hurriedly thrown open, was added the nerve-racking pandemonium of the *Alerte*—the long-drawn Banshee wail of the siren, the piercing notes of the bugle and the clamouring chorus of horns, all intermingled in one insane dissonance.

It was the warning that the Boche bombing machines were coming over the city. *Were* coming? They *had* come, with a vengeance, and their work of fiendish destruction had been completed before their arrival was even suspected.

How had it happened? A guess which I hazarded was confirmed by the brief press report the following morning. With the satanic ingenuity of the Hun in evildoing, two of their bombing *Gothas* had climbed to a dizzy altitude during their trip Parisward, and, when they approached the listening posts which encircle the city several miles distant, had cut out their motors and volplaned over them as silently as any night birds of prey, escaping detection entirely.

They had dropped three deadly torpedo bombs on a district less than half a mile from us, near the *Hotel de Ville*, on Rue Saint Germaine, and had demolished one whole block of store and apartment buildings. A big gas reservoir had also been struck and shattered.

I looked at my companion, and found her calmer than I was.

"Shall I take you to the hotel?" I asked.

"Do you want to go there?" she answered in Yankee fashion.

I told her that I wanted rather to see what damage had been done, and, like a good sport and real American, she said at once that she would accompany me.

We headed in the direction of the explosions, at a walk that was half run. As we proceeded, others joined us; but we did not need their guidance, for now the sky was alight from flames that had shot up with astonishing quickness. In less than ten minutes we had reached our destination.

What a scene of desolation and horror! One whole block of brick buildings had been wrecked; portions of it were in ruins, razed to the ground; other portions, shattered and already afire, still stood; but were on the verge of crumbling. The nearby gas container was blazing fiercely, the ruddy flames thrusting their quivering tongues high into the air.

We joined the scattered but momentarily increasing crowd, many of whom, in every stage of attire, had rushed from neighbouring homes, and directly in front of us was a spectacle to haunt one's dreams. Held with difficulty by five men was a French soldier, stark mad. There was no need to ask the reason, for the word was being tossed from lip to lip by the horrified watchers. He had just come home to find his wife killed outright, and, at that moment, his baby son was on the top floor of the house opposite, which was a mass of flames and every staircase down.

As the *gendarmes* on duty had not arrived, confusion reigned; but representatives of *one* organization were there. The Red Cross was on the spot, ready, as always, to render its varied and glorious aid at a moment's notice.

Everywhere were heard shouts and cries, agonized shrieks, and the sound of heartbreaking sobs.

"Do you mind if I leave you and see if there is anything that I can do to help?" I asked.

"Go," she said.

In company with a Red Cross worker and several civilians, I pushed into one of the burning buildings, and through the thickening smoke until in one room I heard the low moaning of someone in great pain. It was an old woman, partly dressed, her gray locks matted with blood flowing from her cut face, and her breasts horribly gashed by flying glass or falling timbers. I carried her out, surrendered her into the charge of the Red Cross, which had already started a first aid dressing station in a barber shop, and ran back. This time childish cries led me to a room, where I found a little girl not more than six years old. She was lying in her nightgown beside the wreck of her cot bed. Both of her legs were broken just below the knees, and hung limply as I picked her up in my arms. I carried her out also, and this time found the *gendarmes* had arrived to take charge of the situation—quick, nervous, but efficient, little men who, from much practice, knew just what to do and how best to do it.

Quite willing to leave the work of further rescue to them, for I was now nervously if not physically exhausted, I found my companion, and we pushed our way out through the crowd, which had now grown to large proportions, for the neighbourhood was thickly populated with poor people, and made our way through alleys, thickly strewn with broken glass, to the main avenue.

The *Alerte* was still filling the night with its raucous warning, which, as it happened, was no longer needed.

As quickly as possible we found a taxicab, and were driven to the hotel, and, just as we disembarked, the signal sounded to announce that the air invaders had left.

Many people were up, and questioned us eagerly as to what had happened; but I was in no mood to go into detail that night.

I slept mighty little. The city outside was again silent, but in my memory there kept ringing the shrieks and cries of strong men driven mad, of weak women and innocent children shattered and burned. If there had been something of mere excitement-craving in my earlier desire to fly for France, it was that night wiped out utterly.

We may talk about the historic bravery of France, and rightly, for it exists in full measure, but *any* nation would fight like supermen after seeing—not once, but again and again—what I saw that night, and seeing it happen to their own flesh and blood. How can the German mind be explained when it imagines that such fiendish atrocities will shatter the *morale* of a finely bred, highly civilized race? Such a people are not like animals, to cringe and flee before a show of brutality. France and England have not, and we shall not, when our turn comes, as I truly believe that it will if the war continues.

Before I went to sleep I made a silent vow that—D. V.—I would do my little best to avenge a few of the one hundred and fifty non-combatants who had been the victims of Boche bombs that night.

CHAPTER 8

High Spots

I have heard people speak of Paris as still wearing a gay cloak of many colours over a heart filled with black grief. As applied to the real Parisians this is not true, but there is plenty of superficial gayety supplied by the foreign element, especially the soldiers of many nations, on leave or furlough there. These have seen so much of horror at the front that they do not care to permit its shadow to darken the sunlit moments of the rest periods, if they can help it. One may witness a tragedy like that of which I have just written, one night, and the next take part in a burlesque comedy which makes the thought of war being at the very gates seem impossible.

Death by air raiders at night is shocking rather than sublime; but I passed from it to the ridiculous, in one short step during my two day stay in Paris.

It happened in the *Folies Bergères*, which—as everyone who has "done" Paris knows—is an immense and extremely popular theatre and dance hall combined, a conventional stage and pit within, and outside this, a foyer, or promenade, with a wonderful fountain in its centre, and an orchestra in an overhanging balcony. On all sides are tables for those who prefer to sit at their ease and eat, drink and be merry, while listening to the orchestra's music, rather than to take in the show,

A party of flyers, of whom I was one, entered it that night and purchased promenade tickets which also entitled us to enter the theatre and watch the show. Not wanting to miss anything, we took it in before sampling the pleasures offered without.

The show itself was not particularly impressive—all that I remember of it is that it was some sort of a burlesque on a tragic historical happening, screamingly funny at the start, apparently, judging from the general hilarity, but ending as a melodrama. That is, it was intended to end thus, but just when Marie Antoinette—or whoever the fair heroine was supposed to be—had laid her head, crowned with artificial curls, on the guillotine, preparatory to its being severed from her swanlike neck by a very realistic knife, a wild western warwhoop rang out through the tensely still audience. Down the centre aisle, with long, lunging strides, went a big, stunning figure of athletic build and clad in French blue, but obviously an American.

We all knew him well enough, for he was one of the wealthiest and most genuinely popular-on-his-own account men of the corps, a man who was a super-flyer and had already done wonderful work at the front. Here I shall inflict upon him the distinctive name of John Smith, because—as real authors say—that was not his name at all. With a graceful jump, that would have done credit to a deer or a champion high hurdler. Smith cleared the heads of the orchestra; nor did he pause until he had performed a male impersonation of Pocahontas over the prostrate figure of the doomed heroine.

The knife did not fall, so he picked her up bodily and set her squarely upon her feet. This done, he faced the audience, which was now howling with merriment and cheering his valiant rescue to the echo. Suddenly he "came to" enough to realize the absurdity of his position, his triumphant smile turned sickly, and he blushed like a schoolgirl. Then two *gendarmes*, who together would scarcely have made one of him, advanced from the wings and led him gently out of the spotlight, meanwhile admonishing him to try and be a little quieter. Smith offered no opposition, but went peacefully, and we thought that we had seen and heard the last of him for that night. But it seemed that he had only been warming up for the evening's entertainment.

The act ended after a fashion, and everybody, including myself, went out to enjoy the promenade and concert. There was a babel of laughing voices for a little while, then above it rang out the familiar war whoop, and through the crowd of merrymakers burst Smith. He made for the fountain, jumped lightly onto its base and poised like Venus, arrayed in a handsome French uniform bedecked with the medals of a hero. Then, in he went head-first, and, coming up, proceeded to give a free demonstration of all the latest fancy strokes, *à la* Annette Kellermann, with explanations.

His old friends, the *gendarmes*, appeared again and started to remove him; but each time that one approached to the attack he was met with a watery barrage. Frenchmen are apparently not keen for water, so Smith successfully defended his position until he was tired of the game, and decided to come out of his own accord.

When he did emerge his uniform was glistening like silk and clinging to him like tights. The *gendarmes* marched him off in belated triumph to let him dry out and sober up, but Sinclair and I stepped in and supplied bail and took him under our charge.

CHAPTER 9

Lunéville

December third I opened the door to the new life which I had set my heart upon so many months before. I was at last an *Aviateur Pilote Americain*, and a Soldier of France in the newest branch of the old, honourable and world-famous Foreign Legion that had, for generations back, made history in every war in which France has engaged. And I was on the threshold of taking a personal part in the greatest war that has ever occurred in human history.

Escadrille N. 87, I was advised, was located at Lunéville, in Lorraine, two stations beyond Nancy, and so some four hundred and fifty miles south of Paris. I knew, of course, that this particular sector was comparatively inactive at that time; but this fact did not trouble me, even though I wanted to get quickly into action, for I had come to the conclusion that the more experience I could obtain before things warmed up with the coming of Spring, the better fitted I should be to play my part in the "warming."

I left Paris at seven-thirty in the morning to make the fourteen-hour trip on a slow train packed with soldiers returning to the front. As I was pretty well tired out after my long training, capped by my two night experiences, I slept almost all the way to Nancy, which we reached at five-thirty in the afternoon. A half hour for supper at a little restaurant that I was to visit again, and I boarded another train for the last lap of my journey to the fighting front, and arrived at my destination at half past seven.

I had thought Paris dark. What, then, was my feeling as I stepped from the train at Lunéville. It was only ten miles back of the first line trenches, and was, of course, emptied of all civilians except those connected with caring for the army. The houses and streets were all in darkness which would have made Egypt's night broad daylight by comparison, for every door and window was screened, and even the autos which went through the pocket-black streets, "hell bent for election," carried no lights.

Captain Azire of my new *escadrille*, a dark, handsome little Frenchman, who wore the usual pointed black moustache, was on hand to greet me at the station, having been notified of my impending arrival, and, after we had shaken hands, he guided me through the inkiness to my new home. I could not, naturally, distinguish anything about it as we entered; but, as I came to know it later, it proved a homelike, attractive place, utterly different from the rude barracks which had been my portion for many months.

Before the war had desolated the land, our *château* had been the domicile of a French count who, with his family, was now somewhere In the south of France. It was a typical little *château*, square, built of stone blocks, and three stories high. A ten-foot high stone wall, with a now rusty iron gate in the centre, surrounded it, fronting a broad street with pebble sidewalks and lined with old trees. Within the gate was a narrow pebble path which ran up to the big front door, and then branched off and went around one side of the house to the kitchen. On the right of this, in the front lawn, now, of course, covered with snow, was a little fountain, and on the left was a big tree, beneath which we placed small tables and chairs and did our lounging when Spring came, for the house boasted no *piazza*. The nearest approach to such a thing were the diminutive iron balconies outside each of the tall, Venetian windows.

Feeling something like a new boy at school, I followed Captain Azire into the hallway, and to a big room, on the right, which served the occupants as a combination living- and dining-room. It was high-studded, and the light gray walls were bare of the family pictures which had once adorned them, and which were now—in company with the other valuables of the household—safely locked in a room across the hall. In the centre was a big table capable of seating fifteen, and an upright piano. A man in the uniform of a sergeant of aviation was drumming away at it as we entered, and a dozen or so more were lounging about, smoking, chatting and playing cards.

My comrades to be were all French, with the exception of one Russian (three other Americans joined us for a short time, later), and I shook hands heartily with them as the captain presented me to each in turn.

After the formalities were ended one of them took me to my

room upstairs, a plain but good-sized chamber with one big mahogany four-poster and two small cot beds, a large wardrobe, which took the place of a closet, a chest of drawers, commode, three chairs and a varied assortment of trunks and bags on the floor. Of course, there were no modern conveniences, but it seemed like a palace room after what I *had* been living in.

By this time "dinner was served," and I went down to an excellent meal of steak, potatoes and beer, during which my difficulties with the French language were the cause of much merriment and laughter at my expense.

As I was still somewhat weary, and a bit lonesome among all those strange faces, I went early to my room. Outside it was now snowing heavily, turning the darkness to faint gray, and the shut-in feeling, which this produced, increased my loneliness. For the moment, thoughts of home eclipsed my former delight over the achievement of my ambition's goal, and it was in this mood that I went to sleep. Outside everything was as quiet as a country churchyard that night, although more often than not, thereafter, I was to be lulled to sleep by the incessant sound of the distant bombardment, the reverberant booming of the big-calibre guns, the dull crunch of the hand grenades, and even the intermittent sharp rattle of the rapid-fire guns and rifles which combined to form a steady concussion that kept the old house rattling, and made my bed tremble constantly.

At daybreak I was awakened to a sense of unreality and strange surroundings. Then, as the haze of sleep passed from my brain, came the thought that I was actually at the front and about to begin my military career in earnest. I jumped from my narrow cot into the chilly air and looked out of the window. It faced the east, and my gaze travelled over a snowclad, rolling countryside with here and there the shattered roof of an isolated farmhouse appearing. None of the no-less shattered villages nearer the front were visible, however, nor were the opposing lines of trenches—five miles distant.

It was only half light, but the weather had cleared during the night, and, although the snow lay thick upon the fields, the wintry air was still, and I knew that I might reasonably expect in a very short time to make my initial flight under real war conditions. With eagerness to be up and doing, I dressed and went downstairs, and in a few moments was at the front door, ready to accompany my new comrades to the aviation *piste* which lay just across the street. It was a huge, unfenced field which took three-quarters of an hour to circle in an automobile, and was bordered by big gray hangars, each of which held ten machines.

We breakfasted on chocolate and toast at the canteen, and then I reported myself ready for duty to Captain Azire. He called for and introduced François, my mechanic—a short and slender little fellow—and then assigned my new machine to me—a *Nieuport*. It was a beauty, wonderfully camouflaged on the top of its upper planes and *fuselage* with blotches of green and reddish brown so that, when looked at from above, it would blend into the earth beneath. The art of camouflaging airplanes has kept pace with that of disguising almost everything else used in warfare. It is, however, useless to attempt to do much to their under sides, for, against almost any kind of sky, they are visible because of the shadow; but I have seen enemy planes so cleverly "doctored "with varying coloured paint, that, from a thousand metres above, they would pass completely unnoticed, unless the eye chanced to catch the black iron crosses which are painted near the centre of the Boche's wings. As you know, the French *coquard*, or design, is concentric circles of blue, white and red; and the American, a star in a circle.

My new *chasse* plane was obviously the best I had ever had, and, as keen to try its flying qualities as any boy to mount a new bicycle, I donned my winter flying clothes and climbed aboard. She took the air as easily and lightly as a bird, after a "taxi" trip of not more than forty feet over the crusty snow, and, as we soared upward in wide circles, I found, to my great delight, that she was not only swift, but so responsive to the controls that I could almost "breathe" her around.

Oh, the indescribable joy of flying a perfect plane!

I glanced down, saw that the captain was watching me and, just like that boy on his new cycle, began to show off, with all the acrobatic stunts which I had recently learned at Pau..Yes, I was frankly trying to make an impression, and, although I probably failed to thrill him with my exhibition, I at least earned a "*Bien fait, Wellman*," when I finally descended. From a veteran flyer that means more than any lavish encomiums from a layman, and I felt a glow of satisfaction. After all, what more need ever be said than, "Well done"?

"This afternoon you will take your first trip over the lines with our 'ace,' 'Ruamps,'" added the captain. "Ace," by the way, is spelt "As" in French, and pronounced "ass."

I saluted, well pleased, for I was already in love with my little machine, and replied, "*Merci, mon Capitaine, Je suis prêt.*"

I had already determined upon a name for the first plane that

should be really mine, to all intents and purposes, the "CELIA"—
my mother's name—and when I announced it, my mechanic had it
painted in big black letters on the top of the *fuselage*, over the Black
Cat, which was the emblem of our *escadrille*, and which adorned the
side. He also added the numeral "I" which proved to be prophetic. I
was to see four others bear that name with other numerals.

The evening before I had met M. Ruamps, and had heard that
he was a devil in the air, with five Boche planes to his credit already,
downed during six months of flying at the front; but one would never
have guessed his record from his appearance, for he was a little chap
with a smooth, round face almost like a Kewpie's. He was only eighteen years old.

Poor lad, I was to see him killed by my side within two months.

I passed the two hours before dinner-time on the field, and in the
hangars, talking with mechanics, some of the pilots, watching others
in the air, and, in general, trying to become mentally acclimated. Nevertheless, when the dinner hour arrived, I discovered suddenly that I
had lost all appetite, although I had believed myself to be ravenously
hungry. The anticipation of the coming flight over the battle front had
stolen it quite away.

Trying to conceal my nervousness with an air of nonchalance, I
nibbled at my food, but I feasted full upon the conversation, which
turned on air flights, methods of attack and the dangers (?) from anti-
aircraft guns.

Indeed "fighting" and *femmes* furnished the principal subjects of
conversation morning, noon and night.

At two o'clock I accompanied Ruamps to the field, got into my
togs, and then listened respectfully while he gave me my instructions,
saying, "All that you have got to do is to follow me at fifty metres
while I fly in figures 8 over the front line trenches. There'll be no
fighting today. I mean to keep away from any scraps, for I merely want
you to get accustomed to the lay of the land. Get the principal land-
marks fixed in your mind."

I climbed into my plane, François started the propeller, and we
were off. Ruamps' directions had sounded simple enough, for it was to
be merely the old *Vol de groupe*; but I quickly discovered that it was not
so easy to adapt my high speed to his, and follow him at the prescribed
distance. In fact it was so difficult that it took all my concentrated attention, and, when I followed him down to the field later, I knew no
more about the territory over which I had flown and was going to fly,

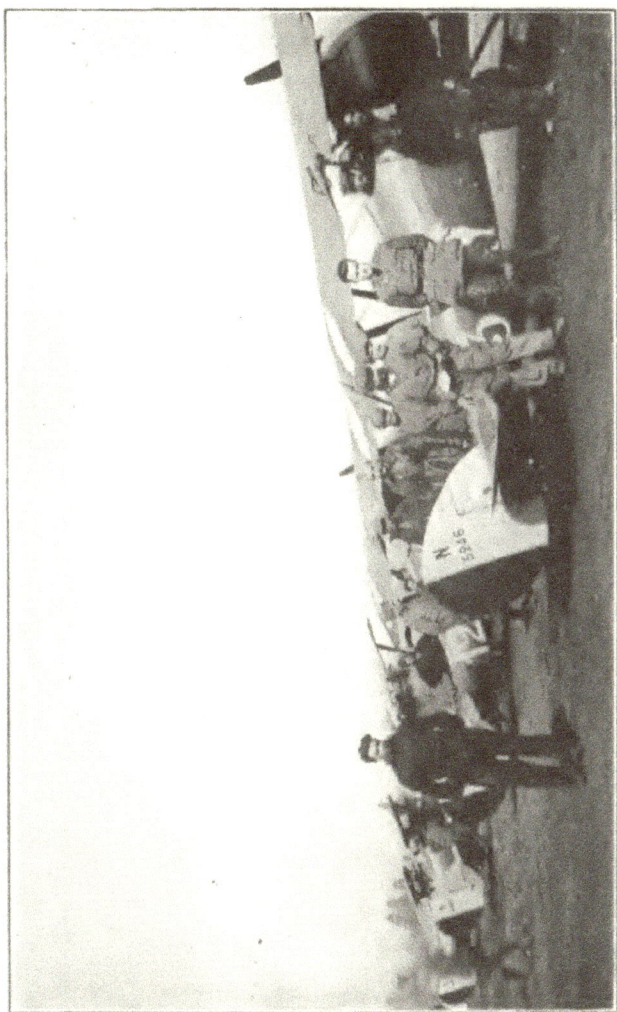

MACHINES LINED UP FOR FLIGHT

than I had when I went up an hour and a half before. My chagrin was somewhat diminished, however, when, in reply to my confession, he smiled and said, "Oh, that was to be expected. You have prospects, and will no doubt made a good pilot in a short time."

Before we reached our *château*, it had begun to snow again, and, as this ended the flying, the others came drifting in shortly. By supper time there was an old-fashioned blizzard raging outside, but within the dining-room all was cosy, and Mirth was King. Indeed, I could not help thinking that the supper was more like an old-time bachelor dinner than a wartime meal, for, although the food was simple, there was wine and song a-plenty.

CHAPTER 10

Flying for France

Five days of bad weather followed, and, with flying out of the question, we spent the time in rest and recreation. The others evidenced no regrets; but, like all beginners, I was restive under the enforced vacation. Part of this period of idleness I spent in getting acquainted with many men of many classes in and about our camp. Among them was our chef, Jean, a grizzly old Frenchman with a sad, weather-scarred face. One day he told me his story, and as I heard it I did not wonder that his yellow teeth were bared while he spoke.

His home had been in an Alsatian village where, before the war, he had lived the life of a peaceful farmer, with an old mother, his wife, two grown-up sons, a daughter of eighteen and one of eight. When the conflict began, he and his two boys had been summoned to the Colours, and had joined different regiments, leaving the women folks at home. Almost immediately the Hunnish hordes had swept over the little village, and they still were holding it. For months, filled with weary waiting and despair, he had heard nothing from home. Then came a letter from his wife, smuggled out.

They were all alive, but they had better have been dead, he said; for they, in company with every other woman and girl in the village, from six years up to old age, had been horribly maltreated by the Boche and affected with loathsome disease.

When I left Jean I was praying for clear weather and a chance to do some little bit toward avenging him and the thousands and thousands of others whose case was like his in France.

Oh, yes, we loved the Germans! We even named places after them. For instance, near Jean's domain was the "*château* of the Crown Prince and Princess." It was our piggery.

During this time of waiting I received word from home that my only brother, Arch, had enlisted in the United States Aviation service. I had commenced by urging him to do it, then shifted, and pleaded with him not to, as I learned more about the hardships of training—in France, at least—and in my letter, written upon receipt of the news, I handed out some brotherly advice which must have seemed strange to him, for he was always the deliberate, careful and efficient kind, and I the harum-scarum, wild one. Yet it was, and is, good advice, and I am tempted to quote from my letter for the benefit of any reader who may someday take up flying.

> The training period is certainly the most dangerous, and, when you start it, go easy and take care of yourself. The big question is as to the strength of the machines; they get such hard usage in the schools that they are liable to be weak. Keep your eyes open all the time, and remember that you are not a 'flyer' until you are actually ready for the front. I went through school fast; but my accidents were all the result of thinking that I was a flyer at the start. They taught me a lesson.
> Just plod along and let the other fellows win the name of dare-devils. Don't try any 'funny stunts' to earn a reputation for yourself—there are plenty of darned fools to do that. Just be the same conservative plugger that you have always been, and you will come through a-flying. I am actually sorry for the words that the captain at school wrote on my certificate, 'a born pilot, but crazy.'

Except for the ever-present *totos*—the French for "cootie"— living conditions would have been almost ideal, and, compared with the doughboys in the trenches, or even in rest billets in the village, we lived like princes. To be sure we had to pay seventy *francs* every fortnight for our excellent dinners and suppers, and this was a heavy drain on my small income, although the rest, who were all sergeants or better, did not mind it. However, brother Arch proved himself a brick, and sent me a monthly gift which saved the day, and I frequently received bully packages of candy, cigarettes and newspapers from my guardian angel in Paris, Miss Wood.

So the time passed pleasantly enough, for the association was more like that of a cosmopolitan club than any army, and the discipline was mild, almost superseded by close comradeship, in fact, for Captaine Azire and those under him in command mixed with us frequently, although they lived in another *château*.

On the eleventh, I was delighted by the arrival of Tom Hitchcock, and we immediately agreed to team up again, and made our plans always to fly together when possible. He was a whale of a pilot, and I instinctively felt that I could trust him in any emergency, which means everything to a fighting flyer. We looked forward to working together in perfect harmony and getting results.

Finally came half fair weather, although a persistent mist made flying at the front dangerous, and we spent most of our time in the air, simply keeping our hand in, doing the acrobatics which had become commonplace enough as far as execution went, but still brought me the old feeling of sporting exhilaration.

On the first really good day I had the pleasure of taking Tom on his maiden trip over the lines, as Ruamps had me, and thereafter we flew together as a part of the morning and afternoon patrols. From that time until the day before Christmas I flew; almost continually; but without incident, and saw few Boche planes, and these at a distance. Life settled into its new schedule and I was up and into my clothes, generally without shaving, before daybreak, swallowed a hasty breakfast of chocolate and bread, with perhaps an egg or two, at the canteen in the hangars, where it could be purchased for a couple of *francs*, was onto the field and into the air with the first flush of dawn, and patrolled in a squadron of six or eight flyers, back and forth, back and forth, over the trenches for two hours. Then came a lay off until noon, which brought the very welcome dinner of stew or steak, sardines, vegetables, bread, coffee and fruit. At three o'clock I was up again, and flew until darkness fell about five o'clock, when the day's work was done and we had the evenings in which to amuse ourselves with "smokes," cards, and music.

I early found the men of my *escadrille* a splendid group of chaps and sterling fighters; but, as is almost inevitably the case, there was one exception. He was not French, I am glad to say, but the Russian, and *he* was transferred, not long after I arrived. Not, however, until he had shown his colours, and one of the others and I had gained the satisfaction of punishing him a little.

It was generally reported that he had a habit of going up in a patrol, but soon breaking away and flying to the rear, to return after the customary period, and tell of the fights in which he had been engaged. One morning another pilot and I determined to block his little game, and secretly planned out a campaign to follow. We all went into the air together and headed for the front. Soon the patrol broke up somewhat, as the planes sought different altitudes, and I saw the Russian turn and head westward. So did my fellow conspirator, who had also been keeping an eye on him, and, according to prearrangement, I made sail for a position behind him on his left and my colleague to one behind and on his right. Then we headed in on him, gradually forcing him back toward the lines. Whenever he would turn to the left I speeded straight at him and sent a stream of shots across his bows, and the same thing occurred when he turned the other way, in an attempt to elude us. My companion was on the job. Together we shepherded him up and down the line for two hours. Thereafter there was no love lost between us.

It was also during this time that I had an amusing, yet humiliating experience on earth. There was a strict rule that it was *défendu* for anyone, except pilots and mechanics, to go out onto our aviation field during flying periods, for the presence of people there increased the dangers of landing. One afternoon one of our pilots had "piled up" his plane upon descending, and, as I came out of a hangar, I saw a man in the long trench coat of the infantry standing out on the *piste*, examining it.

Without a thought, I ran toward him, shouting, "What the blue blazes do you mean by coming out here? Clear out, quick"—or something to that effect, only a bit stronger, perhaps. Not until I was almost up to the intruder did I realize, with a wave of discomfiture, that he was a French general. Fortunately he knew that he was in the wrong, and also could see a joke, for he laughed, and invited me to join him at the canteen, where we pledged each other's health.

The days passed with little to break the monotony, few enemy planes in sight and no serious fighting below in the trenches, although the Frenchmen holding them were daily and nightly getting sniped at, or mildly shelled, by the Hun.

Then, on the twenty-fourth, I got my first taste of what my later diet was to be.

The air was clear, but bitterly cold that afternoon. This, however, did not prevent us from going up as usual, for, if we did not, the Boche certainly would have. He was not, and is not any molly-coddle. I went up in the usual patrol and started a weaving flight back and forth over our three-mile beat at fifty-five hundred metres. My, but it was bitter up there, and, after I had been at it for an hour and a half, I began to be so numb, despite my heavy apparel, that I concluded that safety first required my return to earth while I was still able to control my

86

machine. I accordingly left the patrol, which was occupied in doing nothing, and started downward.

When I had reached an altitude of three thousand metres on my downward path I caught sight of a remarkably camouflaged two-place machine, just below me, over our third line trenches, and headed for Germany. For an instant I thought that it was a French plane, starting out for observation work, perhaps; but the next my eyes caught sight of the two black crosses which proclaimed its true nationality, and I knew that it was an *Aviatik*—one type of Boche plane used for photographing. For some reason or other it had not been observed from the ground, as was apparent from the complete silence of our anti-aircraft guns.

Mine was the only French machine anywhere near it, and *it* was the first enemy plane that I had ever seen so close, or when I was alone. On the moment I forgot all about feeling cold, and, with every nerve a-tingle and my blood surging fast, I swept down into an attack, without pausing for consideration.

I had had the proper manner of attacking a bi-place machine drummed into me over and over, as I have described it. I knew, in theory, that directly behind the pilot sat a second man with a swivelled gun who could fire in any direction except downward, and that, of course, the only safe method of attacking it, was to dive behind it at such a speed that that gunner could not make an easy mark of me, do a "Russian Mountain," and come up at the "blind spot" from beneath. I knew this perfectly, but my wild excitement made me forget all that I had learned. There he was, right below, and it was up to me to see to it that he did not get home from his little picture-taking trip.

With only that thought in my mind, I dove straight at him, thereby giving the gunner a fair target for his stream of bullets.

By every rule of the game I should have been shot down instantly; but the luck, of which I have written before, was with me in full measure, for the gunner was an atrocious shot and "never touched me," although he had every chance in the world. Nor was I any better. I fired six times, in my excitement failing to register a single hit; then my gun jammed, which was perhaps a good thing, for it brought me to a realization of my foolishness and predicament. I had just sense enough to go into a *vrille* as I sped past him.

The pilot of the *Aviatik* turned his machine, and dove after me, shooting continuously, and so doing he followed me down for full two thousand metres. Then, apparently satisfied that I was out of control and that he had ended my brief career, or fearing to follow farther directly over our trenches, he straightened his plane out and scooted for home, unharmed.

My heart was in my mouth when I thought of what I had escaped by bull luck, and, as soon as I had seen him abandon the chase, I, in turn, righted my machine and went for home just as fast as it would carry me. Never had I been half so glad to see my own aviation field below. In fact, I was so overwhelmingly happy, when I went into my final volplane toward *terra firma*, that I clean forgot another cardinal rule of flying, and, as I had on the occasion of my first time in the air, failed to pull my control stick back and so bring the machine parallel to the ground at the moment of landing, with the entirely natural result that I plunged into it nose first.

Six thousand dollars' worth of delicate mechanism was smashed to splinters, and I did not care a rap. I was too filled with sheer joy to be safe on earth again for that, in spite of the fact that my first fight and first big aerial experience had ended in ignominious failure.

"Smashed to splinters"

CHAPTER 11

A "Merry Christmas," and My First Boche

Christmas morning dawned very cold, but as clear as a bell, and, with the snow sparkling on the ground and roofs of the houses, Lunéville looked for all the world like a picture-book illustration of a quaintly foreign scene. But the calm beauty of it, instead of delighting me, made me feel intensely blue and dejected. Although I was a mighty long way from home, and the scene appeared utterly different from any that I had ever viewed in New England, I could not help recalling other Christmases when I was in the midst of my family and friends, laughter, gifts, holly—and mistletoe. A few gifts had come, to be sure, and it was not the fault of my dear ones that the major portion came three months late, but the spirit of Yuletide was utterly lacking. I went downstairs and joined my comrades. There were no "Merry Christmas" greetings, and I was only too glad to get out of doors, through the simple breakfast, and to work.

There was to be no recreation for us, as Captain Azire speedily made known. War knows no holy—or holidays, and the schedule for the morning called us to act as escort for a huge *Letord*—a three-place machine used in taking photographs on a trip twenty-five miles into German territory. Our destination was the town of Saarburg, or rather a spot far up in the air over that town, for troops had been reported coming up to the front from it, and it was thought desirable to obtain some photographic information concerning the lay of the land, and what was going on.

The trip was not to take place until two o'clock, so we had several hours on our hands. There was no churchgoing that morning, however. Instead, the majority of us put in the time at the card table.

At one o'clock came our Christmas dinner, not of goose or turkey with the "fixin's"; but steak and potatoes. Soon after it I arrayed myself for the afternoon's work. My costume consisted of three suits of underwear, three pairs of woollen socks and a heavy winter uniform. When I got out to the hangars this was supplemented by my fur-lined flying combination and helmet, fur-lined boots, a sweater, and a muffler wrapped about my neck, ears and forehead. You can imagine what a stylish figure I cut. Santa Claus was never arrayed like unto me, and it took two of the mechanics to lift me bodily into my machine and strap me in place.

But this was not all of my paraphernalia. My combination suit boasted six pockets, and in each of them I put a modern contrivance, made in China, which served the purpose of the old-fashioned warming-pan. It was a small box, covered on the outside with velvet, and containing a slab of charcoal which was ignited at the last moment by a fuse at one end, and was planned to glow for some time. The six escorting *Nieuports* were lined up, and followed the unwieldy *Letord* as it "taxied" across the snowy field and soared into the crisp air.

Like a flock of Winter birds we circled over Lunéville until we had reached an altitude of three thousand metres, and then, arranging ourselves above, below, and on either side of the big three-man plane, we started eastward, crossed the front line trenches at four thousand yards up in the biting air, and struck into Germany, warmly welcomed as we sped over the Boche trenches by the "Archies" or enemy anti-aircraft guns. These are the objects of much ridicule among airmen, for they next to never register a hit, which is perhaps scarcely strange considering the speed and height of their mark; but they are useful in keeping a hostile plane at a respectable distance up.

The explosion of the shrapnel shells around and below me sounded like a dull grunt emitted by a monstrous pig—a sort of a "*wrufff,*" and once *I actually saw one pass* in front of my plane—a small streak of black lightning, if I can use the expression—to burst in black smoke well above. The Boche below were very generous, and the air was filled with compliments of the season from the *Kaiser*. None of his gifts reached us, but it was scarcely pleasant to have them bursting so near, and I am quite sure that none of us wished him a "Merry Christmas, and Happy New Year," that day.

The flight to Saarburg, and the business of shooting it up with the camera while we circled overhead at five thousand metres, took nearly an hour, and there was nothing pleasant in the experience. If any of you

My winter costume

have ever been for any length of time on the top of a three-mile-high mountain in mid winter, you can guess something of what I mean, then add to that the necessity of keeping continually in flight, and maintaining a lookout for possible enemies bent upon your destruction.

At length the *Letord* turned, and headed for home, its work completed, and I, for one, was not at all loath to do likewise, especially as the weather had already begun to change rapidly for the worse. A nasty cross wind came in sharp gusts that kept me busy with my control stick to counteract them and, as we flew France ward, the sky kept growing momentarily blacker and blacker, while dark, ominous-looking clouds rolled up on the horizon. I was both worried and miserable, for, despite my many thicknesses of raiment, I was getting uncomfortably cold, and I had a strong suspicion that my nose was frozen.

There is a cheerful saying that there is nothing so bad that it cannot be worse, and last Christmas afternoon proved the truth of it to me. Before we had gone half way on the back trail, snow began to fall. The snow, hail and wind increased until it became half a blizzard. The icy particles paid no attention whatever to my glass windshield, but leaped it and bit into my numbed face like innumerable needles. One by one my companions disappeared from view, and I was left alone over Germany in the air which was so thick with flying flakes that I could not see the front of my plane, and only the faintest possible outline of the Vosges Mountains far to my left told me that I was still headed in the right direction.

Flying a tiny *Nieuport* under such conditions is no joke. Being in a small boat in a blizzard is a cinch compared with it, for no matter how the waves buffet your craft about they also sustain it, whereas in an airplane the pilot has continually to be on the jump to counteract a slap by an air wave with his side controls, and if the motor, whose power sustains him, goes wrong—goodnight! In the hope that the going might improve if I sought a lower altitude, and, basing my act on the thought that it could not be much worse, I *piquéd* down to five hundred metres. It *was* worse, the air was more broken up and gusty, and the flying correspondingly more difficult.

After what may have been ten minutes of this sort of thing, I made out the formation of the forest of Parroy—which runs some three miles into French territory and three-quarters of a mile into German, crossing the two front lines—beneath me, in spite of its natural camouflage. When we had left it had been black; now it was almost as white as the ground about it. This gave me the direction of our field, and, after a few minutes more of Dante's seventh circle in Hades, I arrived over our *pièce d'aviation*.

Not, however, until to my other worries had been added that of engine trouble. It sounded desperately uncertain whether or not it could hold out, and I kept up a steady flow of words addressed to it, coaxing and encouraging as one might a faithful old horse who was dog-tired and seemed on the point of lying down by the roadside. To be sure, *I* could not hear my words above the roar of the motor, but they—or something—had the desired effect. Out of the enveloping gray blanket below appeared a flare which I did not understand, but it attracted me as a beacon light attracts seagulls in a storm. It was, in fact, gasoline spread on the snow, and lighted to direct the course of the returning voyagers.

At length I landed. Mine was not an orthodox landing, however. Far from it! The wind had now attained so high a velocity that I did not dare to shut off my motor until the slender wheels of my plane were within a foot of the deeply snow-covered ground. One wheel struck first, sunk into the snow, and my machine went over and over in three complete somersaults.

That was the end of the CELIA II, and when it stopped, smashed to smithereens, and with the back end of the *fuselage* bent around until it almost touched the front, it was with a start of surprise that I realized I was still alive. Undoing my body belt, I slowly crawled out of the wreckage. Others were there to assist me; but, to their astonishment, I shook off their helping hands, and, in utter disgust, waddled home. I had been right about my nose. It *was* frozen, and for more than a week it looked like old John Bunny's.

And this was the end of a perfect Christmas Day!

A new uniform which was made possible by presents from home, and which I ordered the next day, partly recompensed me for my unlovely appearance during the days that followed until my nose returned to normal. For nearly three weeks nothing of moment occurred, either on the ground or in the air. We performed our patrol duty twice daily, except when the weather was impossible, and had occasional brushes with the Boche, but nothing more.

Then came the nineteenth of January, and the first BIG day on my flying calendar.

You who read this can look back to something keenly anticipated and finally achieved, and remember the thrill of supreme delight that followed the achievement; but I tell you that, unless you have downed an enemy's machine in a fair fight in mid-air, you don't know what delirious joy really is.

I have taken part in many kinds of sport, but not one of the others can for an instant compare with flying as a sensation producer, and, when to that is added the mad exultation of a contest that transcends all others, and victory crowns it, well—the feeling simply can't be put in words.

Oddly enough, my first successful fight grew out of another escort trip with the *Letord* which, on Christmas Day, had led me into so much trouble. This time, however, the weather was excellent, although still beastly cold. Again we went over the German lines, the big machine finished its appointed task, and headed home, without encountering trouble. It was well on its way toward France, surrounded by six or eight of us little fellows doing police duty around it, when, looking ahead, I saw a series of black and white puffs suddenly appear out of nothing in the blue sky some three miles above Lunéville. I knew them to be bursting anti-aircraft shells, and fired from friendly guns too, for the Allies use a mixture of black and white powder, and the Germans black only.

An enemy's aircraft was somewhere "up there," and, although I could not spot it yet, I broke away from our group and turned my *Nieuport's* nose upward from the four thousand metre altitude at which we were then flying, while the *Letord*, and the rest of its escort dove for the landing—all, that is, except one which had a two-foot high "7" painted in red near the Cat of the *fuselage*, I knew the plane. It was flown by Miot, one of our daring French "aces." To call his attention to the presence of a Boche I gave the usual signal, moving my control stick rapidly from side to side, and my little craft rocked merrily in its cradle of air.

Miot answered in the same manner to tell me that he was "on," and, although it was no part of our prescribed duty, we headed straight for the scene as located by the still bursting shrapnel shells, he on the right and I on the left.

Suddenly the gunfire ceased. Our friends on earth had seen us going into action. For a moment I looked in vain for the enemy, and then, a hundred metres below, and perhaps four times that distance ahead of me, I saw a cleverly disguised two-place *Rumpler*. Even a practiced eye might well have been deceived, so perfectly did it blend into the landscape.

I knew that a *Rumpler* was another type used both for bombing and taking photographs, and decided that it had been playing the same game as our *Letord*.

For an instant I took my eyes off the quarry to see what Miot was doing. To my equal astonishment and dismay he had already started to dive *directly* at the Boche—a most foolish thing to do, as I have already explained. The observer was making the most of his unexpected opportunity, and was banging away as fast as his *mitrailleuse* would fire. Over the racket of my engine I could hear its spiteful "*clack, clack, clack*," each of which spoke in the language of death. It was but a second more before a wave of horror swept over me, for I saw the top left-hand plane of Miot's machine crumple up. The lower plane followed, torn loose by the sudden strain, and down, down, down he went, in a spinning nose dive with only one wing intact and the other flapping piteously like that of a mortally wounded bird.

There was not a chance in the world for poor Miot, for he was falling, wholly out of control, from a height of more than three miles. A sweep of keen sorrow and a shudder went through me, followed instantly by a gripping desire to avenge him.

Action in the air, with one's plane going one hundred and thirty-five miles an hour, occurs much faster than it can be recounted, and, even as I was witnessing the fate of my comrade, I was diving vertically behind the Boche.

When my plunge had carried me past and a little way below him, I tightened the muscles of my stomach, clinched my jaws and made the sharp turn which I have described. Then I turned my plane's nose upward, gave her the juice, and opened fire when I was fifty yards distant. It was too far for dead certainty, and I was forced to go into a side wing-slip to prevent my plane from passing the Boche in its upward rush, without having the satisfaction of being sure that I had punctured it.

At the same moment I saw another plane flash by me to attack in the manner in which I had. This time my eye caught sight of the number "10" beside the Black Cat. It was good old Tommy Hitchcock, come post-haste to my aid.

As I recovered my equilibrium after falling sideways a little distance, I kept my eyes fixed on the spectacle just above and in front of me, and my heart leaped as I saw Tom complete his "Russian Mountain," go streaking upward and cut loose with his Vickers. It flashed once, and the *Rumpler's* propeller flew to pieces.

I followed in his wake, and, steadied by Tom's presence, fired more deliberately, and had the exultant satisfaction of realizing that this time I had scored a clean hit and silenced the enemy's motor. Even so, he was not out of the fight, for the pilot was skilful, and he had plenty of altitude from which to volplane down to safety behind his own lines, if we could not "get" him first. He was wounded, but his fangs were not drawn, and for a few lively moments both Tom and I went through every conceivable acrobatic stunt in order to keep out of range of his two guns, and save our own hides, without quitting the combat.

On my fourth attack came the long postponed victory. My gunfire killed the pilot instantly, and the *Rumpler* went spinning and twisting toward the earth like a piece of paper, to crash into No-Man's Land, a mass of tangled wood and wire.

Both of us followed it down to within twenty yards of the ground, made a quick turn and sped for home at that altitude, pursued by a hell-hail of bullets from the Boche first line trenches, and hearing the return fire of the French *poilus* as we swept over the trenches.

We reached the field together, the two most exultant youths in creation at that moment, and what a reception was in store for us! The fight had been seen from the *Letord*, its escort, and from the field, and, as we taxied to our hangars, the place was swarming with excited Frenchmen who lifted us from our seats and almost devoured us in their delight, for it was not only a clean-cut victory, but my first. Tom had previously scored his first "kill."

During the excitement of an air fight you feel capable of enduring anything, and not until it is all over do you realize what a drain on the nervous and physical vitality it has been. We discovered that we were quite willing to be excused for the remainder of the day, and go to our rooms for a rest; but in my case, at least, sleep would not come. My mind was torn between two conflicting thoughts, that of Miot's death and my own good fortune. It had been the "day of days" for me, for the "first" Boche can be placed to one's credit only once in a lifetime.[1]

---

1. For this achievement both Mr. Hitchcock and Mr. Wellman received the coveted "*Croix de Guerre.*" The latter's citation reads as follows:
"*Le Corporal Wellman, William Augustus, No. Mle 12274 du 1re régiment de La Légion Etrangère pilote à Escadrille N. 87.*
"*Américain engagé a La Légion Etrangère se distingue comme un pilote de chasse remarquable par son ardeur et son courage. Le 19 janvier abattu un avion ennemi qui s'est écrasé au sol près du Bois Maut de la Croix.*"—Original Editor.

TOMMY HITCHCOCK

CHAPTER 12

Seeing Red

In air fighting, it has become almost axiomatic that battles come in bunches, and, as though to bear out the truth of this theory, Tom and I ran into one of our most sensational experiences on the afternoon of the very next day, January twentieth.

The weather was clear and decidedly chilly, with a strong wind blowing from our lines into Germany, when we went up in a two-man patrol, as was now our custom.

We headed for Nancy, a few miles to the north, and over that city started our aerial quarry, a two-place Boche plane which had apparently been making the most of the clear day to take some pictures, probably in preparation for sending a few more German remembrances, in the shape of bombs or shells, into that once lovely little city, now so desolate.

The pilot saw us coming when we were yet a long way off; but, instead of waiting to give us the welcome of a prodigal son, he straightway headed for home. Our planes were speedier than his, however, and we gave each other the attacking signal and set sail in pursuit—a pair of hawks after a fat hen.

It was a real running fight from the start, and, before we had been engaged in it many minutes, we knew that we had met a foeman worthy of our combined steel. Time after time Tom, and then I, made the prescribed attack, and, as often, the Boche pilot foiled us with a wonderful display of acrobatics—*renversements*, wing-slips, *vrilles* and loops—and all the while both he and his gunner were losing no opportunity to make it hot for us whenever we got within their range. They were both veritable masters of the art of flying and fighting.

All the time we were hustling into Germany, with our normal speed considerably augmented by the strong westerly wind. I would dive, swoop up, fire and miss him, as he met my attack with a perfect defence, side-stepping and countering in the air as a clever boxer does on the ground. It was a glorious contest, and I got so excited that it was not long before I found myself yelling at the top of my lungs. This may have supplied a vent for my overcharged emotions; but it was exceedingly foolish, since I could not hear myself, and it used up valuable energy.

The Huns headed for their own aviation base at Mamy, some eighteen miles behind their lines, and Tom and I stayed right with them every inch of the way. Then, as the realization struck home that they were actually on the point of escaping us, something must have snapped in both of our brains. I know that I "saw red." At that moment there was nothing else in my universe except that Boche machine; nothing else mattered, if I could only get it.

Its pilot planed down towards his field, turned and headed into the wind to make his landing, and we followed close on his tail. The gunner was still firing at us incessantly, but the pilot jumped the instant his machine struck, and ran for one of the trenches which surrounded the place. Over the plane we flashed at an altitude of only twenty-five yards. At length we had it where it could not evade us further, and our two-fold stream of shot riddled it completely. The battle madness still held me in its grip, and, pointing my plane still further earthward, I turned my gun on the trenches. The pilot dropped. Then, only eight yards above the ground, and with motors going at full speed, Tom and I flew across the field, shooting at everything in sight, and pouring our bullets into the open ends of the hangars.

Our attack had been so swift, and so utterly unexpected, that the Germans were paralyzed by it, for, for an instant they stood and stared, probably open mouthed; but, when we pulled up and headed eastward, the fireworks commenced. In a moment shells were bursting and bullets buzzing all around me—hornets whose sting spelled death. Now and again my little plane would wince, and I knew that it had been hit. Finally one of the shells exploded with a flash of fire and smoke just in front of my machine, so near to it that the resulting vacuum pulled me instantly into a spinning nose dive. I shut off the motor, and got out of it almost as quickly as I had gone in, having fallen only fifty metres before I was on even keel and away again. Behind, the rifles and trench *mitrailleuses* were blazing away with a vengeance, and, as I climbed to fifteen hundred metres, the cannonade swelled to the most frightful that I had ever heard.

The wind was now dead in our faces and blowing so briskly that our going was comparatively slow. It seemed to me that the ten minutes which it took to reach home were the longest I had ever gone through, for, as my hot blood cooled a little, I began to realize that we had been playing with death.

Of course no one of our friends had seen the finish of our fight; but, even at the field, they had heard the fierceness of the firing, and the manner of our return also told them that something out of the ordinary had been happening. There was a considerable number, including Captain Azire, waiting to greet us, and they helped me out of my harness and seat. When I got my legs on *terra firma* they were shaking so from nervous excitement that I could barely stand, and had to lean against the *fuselage* of my machine for support. The captain excitedly demanded that I tell him what had been going on; but, although my mouth opened and shut, I could not utter a word, and in disgust he turned away and went to interrogate Tom. *He* was in no better shape than I, having also yelled his head off during the combat; but, after a while, we managed between us to give a patchwork story of our scrap, and Captain Azire told us that we had been very foolish—which we ourselves knew; that what we had done had been entirely unnecessary, and that he was tickled to death.

With some curiosity I examined my plane. There were no less than eighteen holes of varying sizes in the wings and *fuselage*, and one piece of shrapnel had lodged in the seat. The CELIA III was sent to the rear for material repairs, and I was promised a new one on the morrow.

It is difficult to believe history's stories of chivalry in warfare after participating in the present struggle. The Boche has substituted for it barbarism in its most fiendish form; but, although the forces of liberty have been obliged regretfully to fight fire with fire, there is at least a semblance of sportsmanship left in their methods. It is found especially among the airmen, for, after all, the elements of a game still persist when the conflict is between two adversaries fighting in the open, while it is utterly lacking where armies numbering hundreds of thousands are hidden in the ground.

Certain unwritten rules still apply among the Allied air forces, and it is not considered good sportsmanship to kill a defenceless opponent, unless it is incidental to putting his plane out of commission. In the case of the attack which Tommy and I made on the hangars, we were under fire all the time, and it was a battle, as well as a mad exploit; but I shall a little later give you a personal example of what I mean.

Now, it is only fair to admit that in general the Boche plays the game by the same rules. Their airmen represent the best of a bad lot, but, even among them, the Hunnish manner of waging war crops out at times.

One of these occasions occurred in our own sector at about this time, and it still further fanned the flame of our deadly hatred for the enemy.

One afternoon I was standing with others on our *piste*, when, in the air at a considerable distance, we saw five Boche machines suddenly appear and attack a lone French flyer. They were on him like a pack of bloodthirsty wolves, and after a moment the victim fell headlong, out of control, to be followed to earth by all five of the enemy.

We made haste to get into automobiles and speed to the spot where the ghastly tragedy had occurred. The Huns had disappeared, after making their kill; but there, on the frozen ground, lay the twisted wreck of the little *Nieuport*, and fully twenty yards distant the body of the unfortunate pilot.

"*C'est la guerre?*" Yes, as far as the fight in the air was concerned; but it was apparent that the doomed aviator had been thrown out of his machine while still some distance in the air, *and his body had been completely riddled with bullets which could only have been poured into it after it struck the earth.*

You can imagine the black rage that filled us at this sight, so indicative of the most inexcusable vindictive brutality.

From the twentieth of January until the tenth of February nothing of especial interest happened in my flying career, although I went up on patrol duty whenever the weather permitted. At last, wearying of this stereotyped work, I asked Captain Azire on the latter date for permission to pay a call on the enemy's aviation field located at Hatignay, some ten or a dozen miles behind the lines. The permission was granted.

The day was a peculiar one. A field of dense clouds, only fifty metres thick, was hanging low over the landscape not more than eight hundred metres in the air. It was, in fact, just the sort of an afternoon for a pleasant game of hide and seek in the heavens.

I streaked upward from our *piste* and plunged into them from below like a diver in Looking Glass Land, feeling my plane tremble all over as I did so. In a few seconds I had emerged on the other side into the clear air and radiant sunshine. Below me was the field cloud, fleecy white and shimmering like soft wool on the back of a gigantic lamb. Here and there in it appeared irregular openings through which the earth beneath appeared to view for an instant, only to be hidden instantly by the concealing mantle.

But, if I could see earthward through these holes, the enemy below could likewise look up and catch glimpses of me as I passed. I glanced backward now and then to see the cloudbed broken up and the black puffs of anti-aircraft shells bursting fully two miles back of me. They were doing their best to locate me; but their best was a long way short of accomplishing their purpose.

Tracing out my route by the aid of my map, and the patches of country glimpsed momentarily through the openings, I finally arrived over Hatignay, and there found my hopes realized.

The clouds formed the shore of a small atmospheric lake, at the bottom of which I could see a dozen miniature machines ranged in perfect order before their hangars, nine hundred metres below me. Over the edge I dove, shooting down for half the distance, then straightened out as a swimmer does under water, and slid down to some two hundred metres above the field. My descent was so unexpected and speedy that the Boche had no time to train their weapons on me, and it was amusing to see them scurrying to their trenches like rabbits for their holes.

At this altitude I flew over the field, raking the trenches, then turned and treated the hangars and the planes before them to a dose of the same medicine, and escaped scot free.

There was, of course, no way of my knowing how much damage I did, for I was travelling so fast; but it is safe to say that it was considerable.

CHAPTER 13

High Notes, and a Hellish Chorus

On the morning of February eleventh, Tom and I were standing on our aviation field, waiting for the patrol to be ordered up, when Captain Azire summoned us to him, and said, "You two are the only Americans in this sector and, as such, are to be given a special task to perform today—one which will, I think, interest you."

We looked at one another and I saw on Tom's face an expression which seemed to say, "Well, what now?"

The captain continued. "Your President has sent a message to Congress, which is really a note addressed to the German people, and to-day Americans from the different *escadrilles* along the front are to have the unique privilege of flying over the enemy's country and dropping copies of it, printed in German. There are also some in French, which you will drop on our captured cities, behind the Boche lines."

It promised to be a new and rather interesting game, we saluted with alacrity, and asked, "When do we start?"

"As soon as you are ready," was the reply, and we echoed Admiral Sims' historic words by saying, "We are ready *now!*"

Captain Azire bade us accompany him to the *Pilotage*, or office, where our curious gaze fell upon several big piles of pamphlets, some—as he had said—in French; but the great majority in German. For an hour we were kept busy in the role of bundle boys, rolling them up into small parcels and tying them lightly with thin twine.

Then, with two bundles each, of the ones addressed to the French in bondage, we inaugurated the first American aerial post, flying in different directions, as special messengers of President Wilson.

My delivery route took me twenty-five miles into German territory over the towns of Saarburg and Mittersheim.

The day was ideal for flying, clear and almost windless; we could keep well out of range of the spiteful "Archies." Their bark is worse than their bite; but there was no use seeking trouble.

It was great sport. When it came to delivering the mail, however, I found out very shortly that it was quite a little trick to get my notes off successfully and intact. Simply tossed overboard when I was going a hundred and thirty miles an hour, they developed a habit of getting mixed up with my wings, or caught in the *fuselage*; but I finally found a solution to the problem. It was by doing a vertical *virage*, tossing the bundles over when I was flying perpendicularly, and at the same instant kicking my machine around violently so that its tail would not strike them, for my plane would have passed before they had dropped a foot.

Frequently the strings with which they were tied would break, or slip off, in mid air, and the pamphlets would go fluttering down like feathers dropped from the wings of an immense bird.

As it was late when we got back, and the weather had rapidly changed for the worse, and become unfavourable for flying, we postponed our bombardment of the German lines until the morrow, when we started off early with seven large bundles each. Perhaps we may be forgiven for our "*lèse majesté*" in hoping that the Boche would all be "gassed" to death by our missives.

Although we went up to work early, it was a "bad" day, very gray, with heavy, low-hanging clouds scarcely two hundred yards above the ground and the wind was treacherous. Still, we had to fly low anyway, in order to make certain that the pamphlets reached their objective points in the first line trenches, so we "went to it." This time the trip, unlike that of the prior day, was replete with excitement from start to finish. A French plane cannot fly boldly only a hundred yards above a Boche first line trench without "starting something." From the moment that we swung into line above the Huns they began banging merrily away at us with their rifles and machine guns in the trenches.

Even above the roar of my engine I could hear the crackle of running fire beneath me, punctuated with the *whang* of the trench *mitrailleuses*, and the occasional droning whine of a bullet as it passed so near that its hymn of hate was audible above all that mad racket. It seems incredible to me, now, that we could both have flown at that low altitude for several miles through an inverted hailstorm of bullets and shrapnel, doing acrobatic stunts meanwhile, and escape scot free, but we did it. Our machines must have been simply covered with invisible horseshoes.

It was amusing to look back and see the men below and behind us dropping their rifles and scrambling for such of our messages as fell square in the trench.

Tom finished his task a few minutes before I did mine, and, with a wave of triumph, headed for home, expecting me to follow. I hurried to dump overboard the balance of my freight; but, just as I was on the point of dropping the last bundle, I became possessed of an insane desire to "show off"—it was that, and nothing else. So, instead of performing my customary *virage*, I sped upward until the nose of my plane reached the low clouds, turned, dove vertically, and, when altogether too near the earth for safety, did a *renversement* and shot up again in a loop. I had just reached the top of my aerial turn, was flying head downward, and on the point of cutting off my motor, when it suddenly quit of its own accord. The magneto had broken.

If I had been a thousand metres up instead of a hundred, the accident would not have worried me excessively. As it was, I realized that my foolishness had put me into as tight a hole as ever I had been in my life. There was no time to spend in moralizing. I had to act, and act instantly, for being upside down in an airplane without motive power, only a hundred yards above the ground and directly over a trench full of busy Boche, is not a thing of pleasure and a joy forever.

I did the only possible thing, a side wing-slip, and came to an even keel not sixty yards from earth. Bullets were now buzzing busily around me, and for an instant I had not the faintest idea of the direction in which my plane was heading, I had performed my combination stunt so hurriedly. My motor was dead; but, as I coasted downward, I heard the firing behind me and knew that I was still lucky, and going westward. If I had *not* been, I should probably have "Gone West" in another, and more sinister sense, that morning.

My low volplane carried me safely over No-Man's Land, although all the time I was instinctively urging my plane forward with my body and wondering if I would make it, or again pay a visit to barbed wire entanglements. In a few seconds I was safely over the first line French trenches, which I had cleared by a bare few yards, the *poilus* beneath shouting as I passed over their heads, and had made an easy landing in a shell-hole whose crater was big enough to accommodate my machine comfortably.

While mentally congratulating myself on my escape, and saying "You can't beat a fool for luck," I leisurely undid my harness and began to gather up my compass, maps and a few personal things, preparatory to evacuating, when I heard the excited voices of four or five French soldiers calling wildly to me from a nearby communication trench. Since I could still understand French only when it was spoken slowly, and with clear enunciation, their words meant nothing to me; but, from the tone in which they were spoken, I gained the impression that something of interest was up, and that it was somehow connected with me. It was. I had sat in my plane only a second or two more, wondering what was coming off, when I heard the discordant *wheeeeEEEE* of a shell. It passed right over me, landed some twenty-five yards beyond, and exploded with an ear-splitting roar and an eruption of dirt, mud, and stones.

Something told me that it had been sent special delivery to William A. Wellman, and, changing my mind as to my safety, I scrambled out of my machine faster than ever I had before and started a sprint for the communicating trench, that would have done credit to a "ten second" man. As I approached it, unceremonious but friendly hands grabbed me, and dumped me within its protecting sides.

It was not a nice place at all. There was mud and water in generous quantities under foot, and more came momentarily from overhead as other shells struck and burst, creating havoc in the nearby field. The bombardment for my own personal benefit lasted for a solid hour and a half. When it was finished there was not so much as a splinter of my machine left. The Boche must have spent a hundred thousand dollars in destroying something costing six thousand!

Regarded from a distance of three thousand miles, and three months' time, it was a highly interesting experience, but then it did not strike me as such at all. I had been bombed in the air; but it had been as nothing when compared with this. The noise was simply appalling.

When they finally got me back to the third line trench, covered with mud from head to feet, I had a greater respect than ever for the boys who have to stand for that sort of thing day in and day out for weeks. The land may have its advantages, but for real comfort and safety give me five miles in the air every time.

The aviation field had been notified of my mishap by telephone, and an automobile was waiting to carry me home, a very disgusted and crestfallen youth.

Both Hitchcock and I had a "battle of Paris"—as permission is commonly called—coming to us as a reward for our recent exploit, and, with ten whole days of recreation in immediate prospect, I quickly forgot the fiasco in which my morning's work had ended.

Dressed in our party best, we left Lunéville late in the afternoon, and reached Nancy at about seven-thirty. It was dark as a pocket, for the quaint old town, now sadly shattered, is only ten miles from the front, receives a bombing almost every starlit night, and lights—even on automobiles—were absolutely taboo.

Still, it made little difference to us, for sightseeing was not on our program. With the second in command of our *escadrille*—Lieutenant Bachidan, a tall, slender and distinguished-looking young Frenchman with a pointed black moustache—we made a bee line for the best restaurant that the town boasted. Its name escapes my mind, but it was typically French—inside a-glitter with lights reflected from many big mirrors, pewter and silverware hung on the walls, and it was filled with officers and dazzling girls.

The meal was a wonderful one for wartimes, soup, fillet of sole, veal, artichokes, wine, French pastry and *café noir*. I was just paying the check, having been less lucky in "flipping" than I had been in flying, when, above the merry chatter and laughter of the diners, came the conglomerate sound of the *Alerte*—the agonized shriek of the siren whistles, piercing notes of the bugle and honking of many horns. Even to those who have heard it often, it brings a sudden tightening around the heart, for one never knows who are to be the victims of the bombs from the blackness above, whose arrival the *Alerte* presages.

We all sprang to our feet, with the laughter instantly stilled. The logical thing, of course, was to make for the cellar, so we all rushed for the street door, and had almost reached it, when there came from directly outside a sound like a terrific thunderclap accompanied simultaneously by a nerve-tearing like that of the lightning's bolt. The explosion set the restaurant to rocking violently, windows, mirrors and glassware were shattered, the place was plunged into darkness, and some of the girls fainted.

When we reached the open air, we saw merely the still falling ruins of what, a moment before, had been a pretty two-storied stone house immediately across the street.

High above, the stars were shining peacefully, and already misty fingers of light were shooting upwards and searching the darkness. Now and then one picked up a Boche machine high in the heavens— we learned later that twenty had taken part in that evening's raid— and we could see the red and yellow lights of the French planes as they climbed upward to drive off the invaders, and the quick flashes of the anti-aircraft shells bursting around and below the enemy. And, strangely enough, through and above the voices of the guns, we could continually hear the low but strangely penetrating growl of the Boche motors.

This was the fourth night-bombing raid in which I had played the part of a helpless spectator, but I had not—and never have—become hardened to it. The same was true of my two companions, and, like three frightened children, we scurried for the lieutenant's automobile, and made more haste than was consistent with safety for a railway station, three stops down the line. Remember, we had to drive, without lights, over black and unfamiliar roads. Twice, as we were speeding along, I heard the descending whistle of a bomb, one of which burst with a blinding flash and terrific detonation only a little way to our right, and the other farther off to the left.

The sky was now a network of moving searchlights which made silver traceries on the black background, and I had just stood up excitedly in the *tonneau* to point out one of them in whose path a Boche machine appeared like a shimmering white night moth, when I was suddenly flung against the front seat. The driver had applied his emergency brake with all his power, and it was well for us that he had done so, for the car came to a grinding stop on the very edge of a newly made bomb hole fully six feet in diameter, right in the middle of the road. Making a cautious detour around the brink of this crater, we finally reached our station, only to have to wait six weary hours for the Paris-bound train which had been held up by the bombardment. Travelling in Southern France is uncertain, at present.

The first thing that Tom and I did upon reaching Paris the next morning was to call upon Dr. Gros. The call was a highly pleasant one, for it produced not only his congratulations, but checks for five hundred *francs* apiece—a little present from the Lafayette Flying Corps in recognition of our victory.

Thereafter my stay in the city was one continual round of recreation and I fed full on the many pleasures that it had to offer. During it I met several other aviators on leave at our hotel, among them Major Lufberry, then and until his unhappy death, the king of American flyers. He was older than most of us, but he was most genial and wore his honours lightly.

I also ran across Frank Baylies for the first time since his departure from Avord, and we "talked shop" for quite a while. During the

Lieutenant Frank Baylies

conversation he described to me a phenomenal escape that he had recently had. His plane had been disabled and brought down in No-Man's Land, and the Alpine Chaussers who were holding the front line in that sector had promptly put up a triangular barrage between him and the Huns, he being in its apex. Unharmed, he had run and dived into the trench.

"But weren't the Boche firing at you?" I asked.

"Were they? Well, rather, but their bullets weren't going fast enough to catch me as I made *that* trip," he replied.

CHAPTER 14

The Rainbow in Lorraine

My ten days of much appreciated leave came to an end, and on February twenty-first I headed back to Lunéville, arriving in the evening.

When I left the train at the familiar station, I had the odd sensation of thinking that I must have disembarked at the wrong place. Only a little more than a week previous, the narrow streets had been filled with nothing but wiry little French troops in their light blue; now these seemed to have suddenly grown bigger, more husky and younger, and to have changed their uniforms from the colour of the sky to an olive drab. I figuratively rubbed my eyes, and looked again. The same strange sight met them. In every direction were new, yet familiar, types of faces, bronzed, alert of expression, and crowned with soft slouch hats.

My own cap went into the air, and with a wild shout I dashed for the nearest group. They were the *Americans*, the Americans at last, and a strange happiness made my breath catch in my throat. When I had left Lunéville there had been not one in the town, I had heard not even a rumour of their coming, yet now the streets were full of them, laughing noisily in their happiness to be almost in the thick of the fray, and—*talking English*.

Without any trumpeted announcement they had come silently up, thousands of them, to take their places for the first time with their new allies in the front line trenches. Some were already out there in the darkness five miles away, small groups along a three-mile sector, intermingling with the veteran *poilus*, and learning the art of modern warfare in the stern school of actual experience. The others, and greater majority, were still in rest barracks in the town which had been my home for two months, and were fraternizing perfectly with the

French quartered there also.

A strange name it was by which they designated themselves—the "Rainbow Division"; but its appropriateness was instantly apparent, for not only were their hat cords of the various cardinal colours, denoting many different branches of the service, but, if ever a body of men spelt "hope," it was this one—hope for the Allies, hope for civilization and the rainbow promise of the coming of more and yet more to bring the sunlight of victory after the storm.

Perhaps they were not *a sight for sore eyes*, and perhaps I did not talk with them from colonel to cook. Almost immediately I became a frequent visitor at mess with certain of the officers, democratic princes all. And they seemed almost as glad to see someone in the French uniform who could speak *American*, as I was to see them.

To be sure, my association with these splendid men and boys of ours, except when—with an added incentive—I was in the air over the trenches, guarding them from hostile airplanes, was purely social; but, when I was off duty, I both saw a good deal of their life, and heard many first-hand stories of their doings, so that I felt almost like one of them.

Since any word concerning the "boys from home," who are "over there," cannot be amiss, I will tell one or two of these stories and mention a few of "the boys" with whom I became pleasantly acquainted.

Their great commander was in Lunéville only periodically, and occasion never served so that I might have the honour of meeting him personally, although I saw him several times and his name was on every lip. The stories of how his troops worship him are in no wise exaggerated—he is their idol, and rightly so, for he is every inch a man and a fighter.

I did, however, become well acquainted with several of the officers, among whom none stands out more forcibly in my recollection than Major George Emerson Brewer, M.O.R.C, a famous New York surgeon in times of peace, and also a close friend of the Hitchcocks, father and son. Tom and I dined with him a number of times, and I enjoyed immensely his hospitable and genial entertainment.

Another of my new acquaintances was Captain de Forest Willard, a regular army officer, whose home was in Philadelphia. He, too, was in the Medical Corps, and was a recognized expert in bone setting, as well as an authority on "trench feet"—a painful affliction and swelling brought on by long standing in mud and water. For several years, before we entered the war, he had been in England and at the front on behalf of the government, making this a special study, I believe. Under him was a young lieutenant named Dicky, from Tarentum, Pennsylvania, who was not only a clever physician but something even more interesting to us—an accomplished pianist. He would frequently come to our *château* and make the strings of our old instrument talk in ragtime, or the language of the classics in music, for the men who were quartered there.

Two others, who were almost always together, fine young Texans and the best of sports, were Captain Royal A. Ferris, Jr., of Corsicana, and Captain W. R. Hudson of Dallas, both of the motor squadron. I dined with them, or they with me, continually.

From the few localities mentioned you can see from how widely separated sections of the good old U. S. A. the men of the Rainbow Division came. They were not only like a band of brothers representative of the unity of our country, but the highest type of American manhood—the first to volunteer.

No one section had a monopoly of courage; they were all brave and willing, yet it was the white troops from Alabama who first established a reputation for fearlessness and fight, which earned for them the name, bestowed by their French comrades in arms, of the "American shock troops."

Like most things of like nature, it came about as the result of one particular incident, and I mean to tell the story here in all its gruesomeness, for it is a sample of what goes on daily and what America has got to recognize and face squarely.

The story is, of course, hearsay; but I can vouch for its truth, for I heard it first-hand from some of those who participated in the incident, and also saw and talked with the victim.

One night, not long after the Yankees had taken their place in the front line trenches, an Alabama boy was sent out, under cover of the darkness, to a listening post in a shell hole close to the German lines. There, all alone, he was surprised by a number of Huns and wounded so severely that they left him, apparently believing that he was as good as dead. But, before they departed, they mutilated his body with their bayonets in a most brutally horrible and indescribable manner. Six hours later his comrades found and rescued him, bringing him into the American lines, almost, but not quite, dead.

When his fellow Alabamans learned what had been done to him, and realized the wanton fiendishness that had caused it, they knelt about him in the mud of the trench, and took a fearful and solemn oath to avenge him and *never take a German prisoner*. Nor have they, and if you could have seen what I saw, you would have only praise for them.

The German fighter has ceased to be a human being. He is a mad animal—no, he is lower than any animal, for his atrocities are the result of diabolical premeditation, not the mere killing instinct.

Of quite a different nature was another incident that was described to me by one of my new friends, and in which another Alabama boy played the leading role. I met him also. He was a corporal, a huge, light-haired chap, with the mild manners of a baby, and a soft Southern drawl in his voice; but, as often, appearances were deceitful in his case, and he was a "scrapper" from the word go. One night he, too, had been on outpost duty, and, when he rejoined his comrades in rest billet, he told them that he had captured and brought in a Boche prisoner. (This happened *before* the other incident, by the way.) They laughed at his tale and told him to tell it to the Marines. The next night he left the front trench on an unofficial trip across No-Man's-Land through the pitchy darkness, sneaked along until he had discovered an enemy outpost and then, springing upon him, he carefully knocked him out with a blow from his fist. The German was almost as big as his captor, but the latter bundled him across his shoulders, "toted" him back like a bag of meal, and threw him down in the trench with the drawled-out words, "Thar, now perhaps yo'll believe me." They did.

I might go on to tell you many other like stories, both tragic and humorous; but this is a narrative of the air, not the trenches, so I will return to my own element.

For the better part of that week I flew daily over the Rainbow boys without having a chance to engage the enemy in their behalf, but February twentieth produced a bit of excitement which had an unpleasant ending.

The morning dawned clear, with all conditions auspicious for photography, and I was one of seven *chasse* pilots selected to go into Germany as air convoy for one of our big *Letords*, whose observer was instructed to take a few new views of Saarburg. We made the twenty-five-mile trip, flying low at only three thousand metres, from which altitude I could clearly see the countryside with its shining canals, rivers and narrow white roads, as we flew over them. When we approached the city, laid out in dull red and brownish squares, the wispy smoke from its buildings, and the darker smudges from the steam engines going and coming, were clearly visible.

Undisturbed for a time, our clumsy *Letord* circled slowly around until the photographer had taken all the pictures that he desired. Finally his machine headed for France with our little planes on either side, above and below it, and almost immediately I caught sight of twelve speedy Boche *Albatros* machines coming for us from farther in Germany, and they had the altitude on us.

An *Albatros*, by the way, is almost the exact counterpart of the *Nieuport*, except that its wings tilt up a trifle, and they, and its rear *ailerons*, are a bit broader. Our planes climbed better, but they had it on us in diving.

As they dove, I shot down beneath the *Letord*, to protect it at its most vulnerable point of attack, at the same time, to the best of my ability, watching out for the enemy.

In an instant, the air at that spot was the scene of a veritable dog fight. The enemy greatly outnumbered us, but our duty was plain—to protect the *Letord* at all costs.

As I looked upward at the *mêlée*, I saw one Boche fly clear and shoot downward almost vertically, until he was directly beneath me, and ready to speed up and attack the machine that I was guarding. The best defence in the air, as on the earth, is an attack, and I started to dive on him. My position was excellent, and I should probably have disposed of him in quick order; but, just as I pointed downward, my eyes caught sight of another machine dropping past me, in flames. A hasty side glance disclosed the familiar Black Cat of our own *escadrille*, and the numeral "12." It was enough. I knew that our Lieutenant Marin had been fatally hit, and was doomed.

It was merely an incident in the day's work, and I knew perfectly well where my duty lay; but, drawn by the sort of fascination that a candle exercises on a moth, I simply could not help following that torch in its flaming downward rush, and follow it I did, almost to the earth, and close enough to see that his plane was a complete wreck. Poor Marin, he was burned to death long before his body reached the ground, and there both he and his machine were consumed.

My uncontrollable impulse had caused me to lose a clear chance to score against the Hun; but victory rested on our wings, and the attackers were beaten off with the loss of two planes, while Lieutenant Marin was our only fatality. Still, our exultation was dampened by his loss, for he was a fine fellow and a skilful flyer.

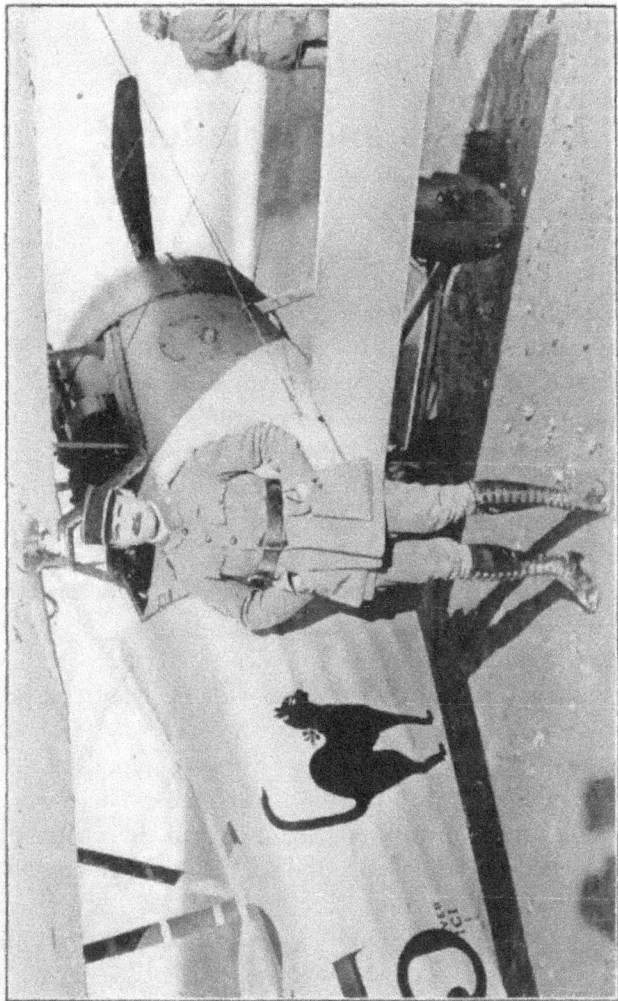

LAST PICTURE OF LIEUTENANT MARIN

CHAPTER 15

Incidents and Accidents

All that had preceded was merely a prologue for the happenings of the month of March, culminating in the sudden—but I trust only temporary—breaking off of my career in the air.

We welcomed the advent of Spring with keenest pleasure. Winter flying is not a thing of joy, and the prospect of better weather meant, moreover, in- creased activity, which was what we all desired.

And the month started off with an amusing incident which set the whole *escadrille* to laughing, and at the same time still further demon-strated the big part that Fortune plays in flying. One afternoon I had finished my patrol and was standing on our field in conversation with Captain Azire. As the air and sky were clear, we could see our boys returning singly and in pairs from a considerable distance.

Suddenly the captain clutched my arm with one hand, and, point-ing upward with the other, cried, "Look there!"

High up, and almost above us, I saw a *Nieuport* coming earthward in a spinning nose dive, with the speed of a bullet. There were no enemy machines about to have disabled it or made necessary such a piece of acrobatics, and it looked as though the pilot had completely lost control of his machine.

"He's done for," I said; "I guess that his rear controls are broken, poor chap."

There was not a thing that we could do to prevent the approach-ing tragedy, and we simply stood spellbound with horror as the doomed plane, spinning like a top, hurtled perpendicularly toward the ground.

It had almost reached its destination, and we were steeling our nerves for the seemingly inevitable crash, when I saw it suddenly straighten out and make a perfect "pancake" landing in the middle of a little stream that bordered the field.

Accompanied by the captain and several other pilots and mechanics, I ran for the spot, and, as I approached, saw that the machine had been badly smashed by its violent impact with the water. Beside it, standing in the icy stream almost up to his waist, was a small French aviator—one of the youngsters of our *escadrille*. He was blubbering like a baby. As we reached the bank and he saw us, he began to say over and over, "*Mon capitaine, mon capitaine, j'etais malade en l'air! Voilà mon appareil!*" ("My captain, my captain, I was sick in the air! Look at my machine!")

The relief from the tension created by the expectation of a terrible tragedy, and the comical sight of the lad with his face a picture of distress and chagrin, was more than any of us could stand, and we fairly howled with mirth. He was helped ashore, and there explained that, while high up, he had been taken suddenly and violently ill with "*mal de l'air*" and had probably fainted away, for he actually remembered nothing more until the plunge into the cold water brought him back to consciousness. Some inexplicable instinct may have made him right his plane at the last possible moment, otherwise his escape was an out and out miracle.

This being sick in the air is not at all an uncommon malady among young pilots. You can imagine what a wrench one's internal anatomy receives when, for example, you do a "Russian Mountain," diving precipitously at a speed of a hundred and fifty miles an hour, suddenly turn almost at a right angle and instantly shoot upward again. Even the experienced flyer gets caught napping occasionally, forgets to tense his stomach muscles, and then . . . "*Voilà mon appareil!*"

Within a day or two of this event there came a piece of news which meant a good deal to me. I happened to be in the *Pilotage*, or captain's office, one morning, when the mail came in. He opened one official appearing envelope, read it through, and then turned to me with outstretched hand, and said, "Congratulations, M. Wellman. I have just been notified by the headquarters of the Eighth Army that your rank has been raised to that of '*Maréchal des Logis*.'" I was as surprised as I was happy.

The title—literally translated, "Quartermaster"—was approximately that of sergeant, although outranking it a little, and it carried an increase of pay, so that now I would get twelve *francs* a day.

At the same time I was also given a still more powerful and efficient fighting machine, a two hundred and twenty horse-power *Nie-*

uport, which carried *three* guns, one, the Vickers that shot through the propeller as in my former planes, and the other two, Lewis machine guns, which were mounted in little pouches on either wing just above my head. All three were fired simultaneously by the single trigger on my control stick, and were so aimed that their bullets would meet, and pass, at about two hundred yards distant.

The next incident of this month, which fairly bristled with them, had a different ending from the one first described, and it cast a spell over the whole *escadrille*. It affected me terribly.

I have already written repeatedly of Tommy Hitchcock, for his brief career and mine were closely interwoven. We had become fast friends while at Avord, and, although he had not graduated until after I, it was only because he entered the school somewhat later, for he beat my record in going through the training, and established one which no other American has ever equalled.

After he came to Lunéville we flew as team mates almost constantly, as you have seen, and, since he was the only other American in our *escadrille* most of the time (Nordoff and Thompson were with us for a while, but had been transferred to Manoncourt several weeks previous to this), we became chums who were as close as brothers. What a flyer and fighter he was—a sure "ace" in the making, although his record was then only two official and two unofficial planes.

On the sixth of March, for some reason which I do not know, he left the platoon and flew off alone into the enemy's country. Probably he had sighted a Boche inviting attack, one that had not been seen by any of the rest of us—and I was not with him! Just what actually happened I have yet to learn, although I may some day; but night came and no Tom Hitchcock, nor could any word of him be obtained from the front line observation posts, to all of which we anxiously telephoned. He was set down among the missing—dead, or, what is often worse in this war, captured by the Huns. I spent a blue and most unhappy evening.

It was not until sometime later that we received word, through a brief note, that Tom had been brought down in a fight near Hatignay, shot through the stomach, and was in the hospital prison camp.[1]

---

1. On May twenty-ninth Mr. Wellman received a letter from Major Hitchcock, saying that he had received word that his son Tom was in Geissen, and had been wounded through the thigh, and later one saying that General Pétain had commissioned Tom as a *sous-officer*, which would result in his transfer to a better prison camp.

With Tom gone I felt lost myself, for we had flown so much together that I had come to depend upon him, and I trusted him absolutely. I knew that if I made an attack, and got into a tight fix, he
would be right there to lend me his aid, and knowledge of this kind
helps greatly in flying. Not that I had any reason to believe that any
one of my other comrades would not do as much, but the feeling still
persisted, and shortly after Tom's disappearance I asked, and received,
permission to fly as a one man patrol thereafter, except when we were
called upon for special squadron duty.

It seemed almost ironical to me that I should be *the only American*
in the air over the lines held partly by American troops, for more and
more of the Rainbow boys were being graduated daily from their
final training and sent forward to hold an ever increasing part of the
front trench, flanked by the veteran *poilus*.

There was little time allowed me cither for regret or reflection,
however, for Tom's loss came on the threshold of a new series of lively
occurrences in which I had a part, the first of them happening on the
very next day. It came within an "ace" of being my last fight!

For several days past the observers had seen a speedy German *Albatros* flying in our sector, and everything pointed to its being the plane
of the wonderful Boche ace, Geigl, for its nose and the last half of its
fuselage were painted a brilliant red, and it was obviously operated by a
master's hand. The Germans usually camouflage their machines cleverly; but many of their best pilots paint them in glaring colours and
fantastic designs, apparently out of pure bravado, for of course they can
easily be spotted and recognized.

The plane in question, the reports said, always flew alone and at a
high altitude and its owner was apparently out "looking for a fight,"
his method of procedure being to catch a Frenchman flying "solo,"
and suddenly drop out of the clouds upon him. We had all expressed
a keen desire to accommodate him with a scrap, and in me the desire now burned doubly strong, for I was bitter over Tom's fate, and
wanted to wreak vengeance on the Boche.

With such feelings in my heart, I started out on the morning of
the seventh and headed northward toward the spot whence Geigl had
been previously reported. Although I was eager to meet him, I went
with no spirit of superiority or overconfidence. Do not, for an instant,
harbour the idea that the German airmen are inferior as a whole to
those of the Allies. Such is far from true. We may have control in the
air in most sectors by outnumbering them; but, with the possible ex-

ception of that in the Royal Flying Corps, the average skill is as high among Hun aviators as among those of any other nation, and their leading "aces" are flying fighters of remarkable prowess. Geigl was, I think, accredited with twenty-eight allied planes at this time.

Perhaps I should qualify the foregoing by saying that it was true of the time about which I am writing. I am confident that when our Yankee aviators are fully trained in great numbers, they will lead all others in the air, individually and collectively.

When I reached the locality toward which I had headed, I began to fly about, somewhat aimlessly, in a sweeping figure 8, combined with "Russian Mountains," for there was apparently nothing of a hostile nature anywhere about.

After some minutes of this sort of thing, during which I got to thinking about a variety of matters not in the least connected with fighting, I chanced to glance above me. My heart gave a wild leap. There, diving directly on me like a plummet, was the very plane I sought, and it was not a bit more than a hundred and fifty metres over my head! In other words, the German terror had me exactly where he wanted me. I knew that I had fallen into his trap, and the unpleasant thought flashed through my mind that my time had come, as sure as shooting. There was not a second for consideration. By instinct merely, I tilted my *ailerons* and caused my plane to fall into a right hand wing-slip. Instinct saved me.

It is a rather odd fact that when an opponent does a wing-slip below you, it is at first almost impossible to tell in what direction he is tilting, and which way his machine will fall. Geigl apparently guessed wrong, for he sped by me at a widely diverging angle, firing into space.

I was at the time well inside the French lines, and he did not seem to have a very keen wish to engage in battle at a low altitude over the enemy's country, for, when he realized that he had missed me, he turned and headed eastward immediately. I righted my plane, took a few ineffectual pot shots at him, and then turned homeward, quite well satisfied to have come through alive, although I could not say that I had "met the enemy and he was mine."

I did not have time to be frightened during the brief encounter, but I had plenty afterwards, and the cold perspiration broke out all over me when I thought of what I had escaped, again by pure luck.

The very next day brought another and new adventure, from which I drew much experience, but no more laurels than I had in my encounter with Herr Geigl.

I awoke to find the weather most disagreeable, with a bank of heavy clouds covering the earth at not more than a thousand metres' altitude, and I anticipated at least a morning when the "no school" signal would be given. I had guessed right, and for the better part of the day we spent our time in the usual manner, waiting for it to clear up.

About four o'clock in the afternoon, when I was out on the field, I saw two German *Drachens*, or observation balloons, slowly arising from the earth in the distant east, five miles or perhaps more behind the Hun third-line trenches. They went steadily up and up until they seemed to come to rest with their backs against the clouds. I knew, of course, that they held two observers each, and that they were connected with the ground by wire cables attached to motor windlasses mounted on trucks.

It was a fairly ordinary occurrence to see these "sausages"—as we called them—in the sky, and I was turning away, without giving them a second thought, when Captain Azire came briskly up, and said, "Wellman, I want you to go up and attack that right-hand balloon. Have you incendiary bullets in your plane?"

My answer was in the affirmative, and, hastily getting into my machine, I headed upward and eastward; by the time I had reached the front line of Franco-American trenches I was ready to pop into the bank of dense clouds. With one final glance in the direction of my intended quarry, I pulled my control stick and dove headfirst into their soft, moistly enveloping bosom. It is almost impossible to describe the sensation of flying *within* the clouds. There is a feeling of being stifled, all idea of direction disappears, and it is actually impossible to see the front of your plane. If you can imagine yourself being wrapped in a huge mass of light gray cotton wool of a consistency much denser than the thickest fog which you have ever known, you will have it.

The theory of fighting among the clouds is simple enough. You merely estimate how long it is going to take you to reach a given point, judging your direction as best you can, and then pop out again when you think that you have arrived.

But the practice is quite another thing. For a few minutes I flew through the "light darkness," then headed downward to peek out like a mouse from its hole.

I saw my balloon, all right—it was fully five miles behind me, and to my left, which was rather discouraging.

Unseen from below, I hastily re-entered my protecting mantle of

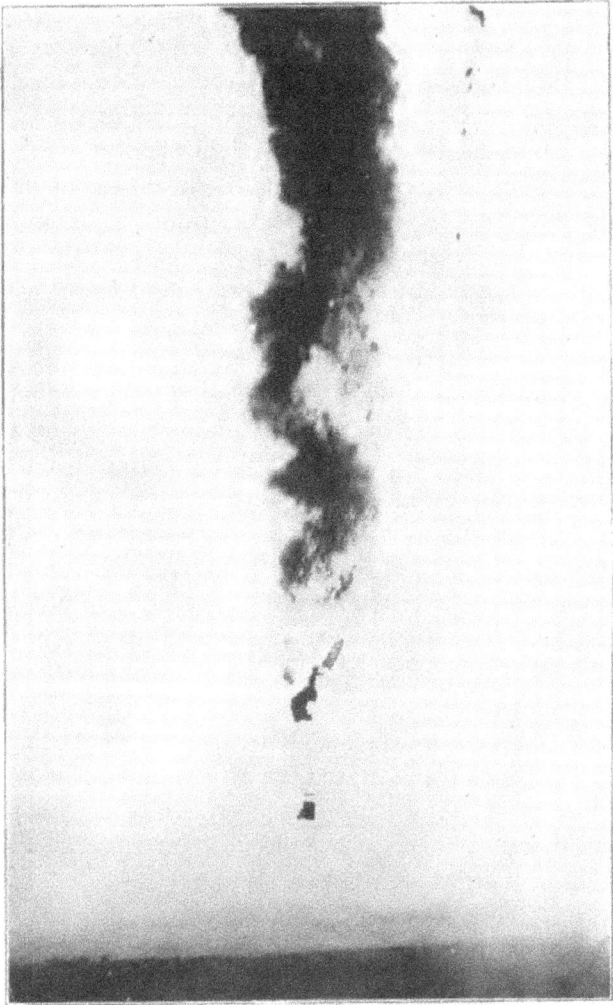

ENEMY OBSERVATION BALLOON FALLING IN FLAMES

invisibility, swung about and tried again. When I was quite sure that I had covered the distance which intervened between the sausage and me, I nosed downward and peeked out once more. This time I was not a particle over three miles off in my calculations, and, swearing roundly at myself, I headed upwards to resume my seemingly hopeless game of blindman's buff. Twice more I made my airy *reconnoitrance*, each time emerging a little nearer the unsuspecting enemy, and on my fifth attempt my judgement was faultless and I came out squarely on top of him. The only trouble this time was that when I shot out of the cloud I could not see a thing but *more* clouds, and it was some seconds before I discovered, to my great surprise, that *I was flying exactly upside down.*

This will probably seem almost incomprehensible to you, but it is a well-established fact that, no matter how good an equilibrium test a man may have passed, he has no way of knowing in which direction his head and heels are pointing after he has flown in the clouds for some time, until his eyesight comes to his aid. Centrifugal force and the speed of his machine almost completely overcome gravity.

I righted myself as soon as possible by doing a quick turn, and dove in a beautiful position, but I was too late. I had been observed, the balloon was rapidly being pulled down by its windlass and, as I neared it, shooting as fast as possible, I saw the two observers jump into space with their parachutes. Down they floated, as unconcernedly as performers at a picnic, and, although I might have killed them both in the air, I refrained, for they were unarmed and helpless, and the French and Americans do not make war on such.

My incendiary bullets failed to do any damage to the sausage, and an instant later I found myself too busy extricating myself from an unpleasant position to bother with it further, for the Huns on the earth below now began to shoot at me with chains, on either end of which were flaming balls of pitch. If one of these had struck and wrapped itself about any part of my plane, I would have reached the earth in the guise of a meteorite. They came too close for comfort, but did not score a hit, and once more I was obliged to start homeward in complete disgust. Captain Azire had been watching me, and soothed my wounded feelings somewhat by telling me that it was not at all a simple matter to "get" a balloon, that I had done reasonably well for a first attempt, and would have better luck the next time.

As for me, I sincerely hoped that there would be no "next time." I would rather attack a whole flock of airplanes than one sausage, after that experience.

The day which followed, March ninth, was to be the day of days in my flying life. The fireworks started early. It was a beautifully clear morning and I started off on a solo patrol soon after daybreak, flying about fifty-two hundred metres high. Not long after I went into the air I began to see shells from our anti-aircraft guns bursting to my left over the forest of Parroy. I *piquéd* down to discover what the excitement was all about, and soon caught sight of an enemy's bi-place observation *Rumpler* over the woods. Mine was the only French plane in the neighbourhood, and, knowing that the Hun was doubtless carrying away some perfectly good photographs of our positions in that sector, and that it was my duty to see to it that they were not delivered to the man who plotted the artillery fire, I got busy. Performing the prescribed attack instantly, I got within fifteen yards of the bottom of my opponent's plane before opening fire on it, and my first shot must have killed the Boche observer instantly, for his body fell half out of the *fuselage*, held in only by his straps.

My upward momentum carried me well above the *Rumpler*, but I felt that I had it, for I had evened the odds and reduced it to a one-man plane, so I turned with the intention of diving directly on it. But just at that instant I caught sight of no less than five *Albatros* planes diving straight for me out of the German air. In my excitement I had not seen them before, and now, deciding in favour of discretion, I turned my dive into a *renversement*, escaped their first charge by scooting upward, and skipped for my home field.

The enemy escaped, to be sure, but he was minus one-half of his personnel.

BRINGING DOWN A HUN

CHAPTER 16

Over the Rainbow

Have you ever experienced an indescribable feeling that something unusual is going to happen soon, that brings with it an unconscious quickening of the pulse? I had it all that day, although there was nothing to account for it. After my return from the morning's scrap Captain Azire excused me until mid-afternoon, but said that we would go up in patrol at four o'clock, as usual. There was nothing in his words or manner to indicate that at that hour my compatriots were going to make their first "over the top" assault on the entrenched Boche, nothing to give me an inkling that this was to be the memorable day when the Yanks would take their first stride in the march to Berlin.

We all knew that the day was approaching; but not that it was at hand, until a quarter of an hour before the time when we were to go up for our afternoon police work.

At three-forty-five Captain Azire came up to me as I stood on our *piste*, waiting for the hour to arrive, and said in the quick, decisive manner of a French officer, "Wellman, at four o'clock there is to be an attack on the German lines and the American troops are going to take part. You are to fly as leader of the lowest patrol at one thousand metres. I am giving you eight other machines and our own second patrol will be just above you. There will be still other patrols from all the flying groups of this sector at all the prescribed altitudes up to six thousand metres.

"*These are your orders. Under no conditions will you allow an enemy's machine to fly over the French and American lines! If they attack, and your machine gun jams, ram your opponent!*

"You will start in five minutes."

I saluted, and he turned quickly away.

Even now the memory of that afternoon is distinct in my mind, down to the smallest details. I know that, when he left, I had a peculiar feeling inside. It was not wholly because of excitement, or from thought of the importance of the task which had been assigned to me. It had something of both of those things in it, and, added to them, was the uncomfortable knowledge that, if my gun *did* jam, the coming flight would be my last. It could have only one outcome—a dead Boche, and a no less dead Wellman.

Sensing that something unusual was up, all of the men of my patrol had gathered nearby while the captain was talking to me. I called them together, repeated the orders which I had just received, and added, "I will fly as usual"—which meant that I was to lead and they to follow in a *vol de groupe*, each one fifty metres behind and above his predecessor—"I will make my turns slowly and rely on the customary signal when about to attack. One thing more. Under no circumstances are any of you to attack until I give that signal."

They nodded silently, and each went to his machine.

I had now risen to the estate of having three mechanics, and with their aid I donned my combination flying suit and helmet, and got into my plane, now the "CELIA V." One of them strapped me securely into my harness, and by that time Captain Azire had approached again and taken his stand before the row of nine machines, which stood like race horses before the starting line.

"*Vous êtes prêt, mon Maréchal des Logis?*" he asked of me.

"*Oui, mon Capitaine.*"

He nodded. Our several mechanics sprang smartly to the propellers and yelled, "*Coupé!*" All of us pilots cut our motors, and reduced the gasoline.

"Contact!"

We gave them the spark and increased the juice. The mechanics gave the nine propellers a whirl and they ceased to be two thin blades of wood and became misty circles.

While two of my men still held the wings I tried out my engine, and found it ready. All the others were doing the same, and the air was vibrant with the whirr and clatter.

A command, even if it had been shouted in stentorian tones, would not have reached my ears, but I kept my eyes fixed on the commander. He waved his hand, my mechanics removed the blocks from beneath the wheels of my plane, jumped aside, and I taxied away across the field, pulled back on my control stick, and glided lightly into the air.

The others followed, and, by the time I had reached my prescribed altitude, and the second line trench, they were arrayed behind me in battle formation. Then I throttled my motor down until I judged by its sound—I seldom looked at the indicator which recorded the number of the propeller's revolutions—that I was creeping along at a snail's pace of about a hundred miles an hour, and then began my three-mile patrol back and forth, back and forth over the line.

High above, the sky was the cloudless pale blue of early Spring—almost the colour of the uniform I wore. In its mystical transparency it faded away into an infinity which made the little things of cloth, wood and wire seem puny, insignificant. Nevertheless the void above my head was now almost black with them, flying in files, and circling like flocks of migratory birds, eight a thousand metres over me, eight more another thousand up, and so, up and up, until I could see the topmost group nearly three miles in altitude, mere black specks against the blue.

Below, a thousand yards, lay the far-stretching fields of glorious France and inglorious Germany, soft green in their new verdure, except for the innumerable ugly, dark scars from recent wounds. To the north, east and west they faded away into the dimly distant horizon; to the south they were walled in by the snow-capped Vosges Mountains, sparkling in the sun, sinking rapidly in its journey westward.

From my low altitude I could clearly distinguish the historic little gray villages, now sadly shattered and desolate; the roads, despite the camouflage over them which was well calculated to deceive enemy birdmen who were flying high enough to be out of range of our anti-aircraft guns; and our first, second and third line trenches, stretching north and south like narrow black ribbons, carelessly unrolled.

In the first line, just beyond where I was flying, appeared our boys and those of our ancient ally, looking like the tiny tin soldiers of babyhood days. At that height I could not distinguish them apart; but I knew that the Yanks held about one mile in the centre, and that the *poilus* flanked them on either side.

Eastward I could see other parallel lines of black—the German trenches. All was motionless there, and no hostile airplanes were in sight.

Indeed, I felt that, if I were to cut off my motor, and the pilots of all the other planes behind and above me were to do the same, the calm and silence would have been like that of a Sunday morning at home in old New England.

Suddenly, just as the hands of my wrist watch reached the hour of four to the dot, the shell-scarred fields below, and to the west, were filled with flashes of flame, belched forth by guns concealed within those ruined villages, shell holes, and clumps of what had once been living trees. I could not see the guns themselves—more camouflage—nor could I hear their crashing detonations over the racket which my motor was making, but I knew that the preparatory barrage had begun; that soon the tiny marionettes below would be on their fateful way across No-Man's-Land.

The thought that the boys from home were about to receive their baptism of fire in an over-the-top attack made my heart beat faster.

This, however, was not all that I was thinking as I led my patrol leisurely back and forth while the shells flew by beneath. I remembered that I was *the only American in the air* at that time and place, and it was with a feeling of deep regret that I considered this. Only one American serving as the air guard for the Americans as they went into the test battle, and he in a French machine, a French uniform, and fighting under the Tricolour, and not the Stars and Stripes!

There was not long given me for such deliberations. One instant the eastern air was clear to the horizon; the next I saw a cloud of black specks, like a swarm of flies, mounting into the sky over there. Little by little they grew larger, assumed the form of airplanes, and the mass separated into detached groups at altitudes corresponding to ours.

It was the Boche!

Their several platoon leaders reached the second line of German trenches, a thousand yards distant from us, and turned as we had. Now they fell into step with us. Two minutes, that seemed like as many hours, passed, and still they flew back and forth in lines paralleling our own. I waited tensely for the moment when one of them should have the nerve to break away from the procession and start the attack. That afternoon we were to defend merely.

It happened! A big bi-place *Rumpler* broke suddenly from the lowest group directly opposite me. Closely followed by a protecting escort of six deadly little *Albatros* planes, he headed toward our lines.

The gauntlet was thrown down. It was up to me to accept the challenge.

I gave the signal by making my craft rock from side to side rapidly, and dove, with my eyes fixed on the leader. He was mine; the others of my patrol by common consent turned their attention to the escort. I flew past the *Rumpler* in a vertical dive so fast that its gunner had not a chance in a million to "get" me, then swung into a sharp "Russian

131

WELLMAN IN THE COCKPIT OF A CAPTURED GERMAN RUMPLER

Mountain" and sped up at its "blind spot," faster than any arrow. The battle madness seized hold of me, and, with my senses in its exultant grip, I pressed the trigger when the Hun plane was only fifteen yards above me, and three converging streams of steel poured into it. I passed like a flash; but not before I had seen his gunner drop with hands dangling over the side, as had my victim in the morning.

The Boche was doomed; but I was not in at the kill alone. As I sped skyward I saw the dark flash of another *Nieuport* diving on it, and by the number knew that it held Ruamps, one of my French comrades, and I knew, too, that he had disposed of his first adversary, and had come to help me with the more powerful machine.

Ruamps' gun spit fire, and, on his first attack, he killed the pilot. As I turned my plane, and glanced downward to determine my position before making another attack, I saw the *Rumpler*, already in flames, tumbling over and over earthwards. Into No-Man's-Land it crashed, to direct no shell fire against our boys that day.

The end of my first attack had left me at eight hundred metres' altitude, flying free, and—looking about me—I saw another Boche just below *and headed into France.*

The words of my orders echoed in my mind, "Under no circumstances will you allow an enemy's machine to cross over the French and American lines."

Pulling on my control stick, I shot upwards to gain more altitude, performed a *renversement*, and was in a perfect attacking position above my new opponent. He must be downed, immediately. I was on the point of starting my dive when, behind me, and above the deafening racket of my own motor, I heard a rapid *"clack, clack, clack,"* like the quick clapping of hands. I knew the sound. It was that of a *mitrailleuse* , and the question as to whether it was mounted on the plane of friend or foe was speedily answered, for a streak of flame flashed past my machine, just to the left. The Boche that shot that "tracer" bullet had almost got my exact range.

A hasty glance over my shoulder showed him to me, diving almost vertically toward the tail of my machine. There was not a fraction of a second to be lost. He had me, just as Geigl had, and, profiting by my previous experience, I went into an instantaneous side wing-slip. The *Albatros* passed me like a shot, did a vertical *virage* and headed for home.

I was safely out of the trap, and, as my other enemy was still below, and a quick survey of the air above showed me that I had nothing further to fear from that quarter, I made my postponed dive.

I reserved my fire, so as to make a sure thing of it this time, and I was within twenty-five feet of him before he saw me coming. Then he showed his skill by diving perpendicularly in turn, and, as soon as he saw that I was following, pulled his machine up into the beginning of a loop-the-loop. Perhaps he thought that I would be caught by this trick and pass below him so that he could get *me* from above, and behind, at the finish of his turn. If so, he was wrong. I doubt if I have ever been so quick to think and act as I was that afternoon under the stress of the battle, and, as soon as I saw him turn upwards, I did the same and looped after him.

When he was at the top of his turn, flying head downward, and I was speeding up from beneath, not quite upside down myself, but with the nose of my plane pointing dead at him, I pressed the trigger. My three guns belched their intermittent fire, and, as I rushed past the Boche, I saw him, quite clearly, crumple up in a heap, the expression of hate frozen on his face. Out of control, his plane went spinning down, and fell, a tangled mass of wreckage, almost in the American first line of trenches. Righting my own plane by means of the useful wing-slip, I surveyed the scene about me. Flyers there were, everywhere; but they were all French and most of them bore the Black Cat insignia. The enemy was vanquished, completely beaten and fled.

I checked my motor and glided gently down to a level of a bare three hundred metres above the battlefield, where I could watch what was happening below, in safety, for the barrage had ended.

Just beneath me was a long line of broad brimmed steel helmets of dull yellow. A little farther to the left the helmets were smaller and changed their colour to dull blue. I saw the diminutive figures clad in khaki and horizon blue scramble out of the trench and start eastward over the torn-up ground of No-Man's-Land. They seemed to me to move, oh, so slowly. Their pace appeared suicidal. Here and there the sun glinted on a gleaming bayonet and I caught the tiny flash of light.

The Yanks, and their brave allies, the *poilus*, were on their way into Germany, and I devoutly wished them the best of luck on their trip

My companions and I had done our little bit; the air was clear of hostile planes; and the rest was up to them.

For a moment or two I watched the strange game taking place on the checker board below, gripped by the fascination of it; but then a glance at my dial showed me that my gas was getting dangerously

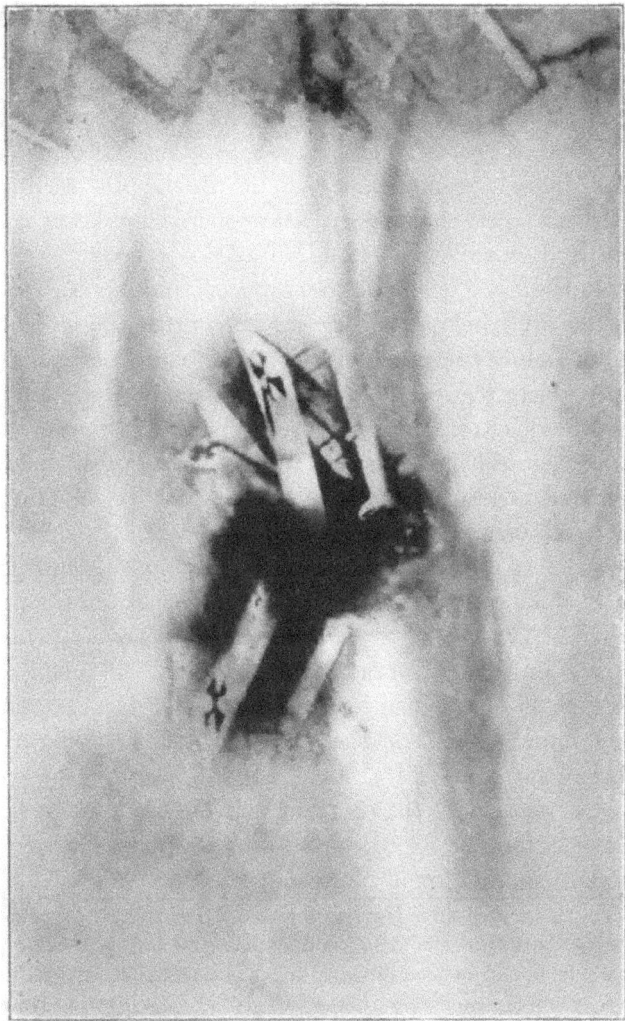

"Out of control, his plane went spinning down"

low and I regretfully turned the nose of my plane westward in a wide circle, and headed for home.

Others were doing the same. The game was over, as far as we were concerned. As I landed. Captain Azire came towards me at a walk that was more than half a run, and, before my mechanics could help me out, he had grasped my hand and said that he had already received word by telephone that an observation balloon and two observers, near the front, had reported that a *Nieuport* bearing a Black Cat and numbered "10" had brought down two machines during the fight. "Number 10"—as I need scarcely tell you—was the "CELIA V." Ruamps had accounted for another and a fourth Boche paid the final toll. But one French airman had been called upon that afternoon to sacrifice his life, and *Escadrille* N. 87 had suffered no casualties.

It was a great day, a wonderful day for us all, and especially for me; but I was too overwhelmingly happy, and too tired, to respond to his words of congratulation, as he wrung my hand again and again.[1]

At seven-thirty that evening, while we were having a dinner in celebration, with champagne in honour of the day's achievements, and all of us were as happy as boys at home after a football victory, an orderly entered, carrying a piece of paper, saluted Captain Azire, who was dining with us, and handed it to him.

He glanced at the message, smiled happily, and—calling for silence—read aloud the words, "The French and American troops have this afternoon taken *three* lines of the enemy's trenches."

There was a mad outburst of cheers and yells. We all sprang to our feet and began an Apache dance; but he demanded silence again, and read an additional sentence, "*The Americans conducted themselves in a most courageous manner.*"

Again the chorus of yells rang out, and this time my voice was raised above all the rest, for the boys of the Rainbow Division who had been tried and not found wanting.

---

1. As a result of his achievement in bringing down two planes within a few minutes of each other on the afternoon of March ninth, Maréchal des Logis Wellman received another gold palm leaf on his *Croix de Guerre*, and the following citation, which included recognition for two victories won previously: "*Le Pilote Americain Maréchal des Logis Wellman, William Augustus, pilote de chasse, montrant les plus belles qualités d'audace et d'ardeur offensive.... Le 20 Janvier, ayant pris un bi-plane ennemi en chasse au-dessus Nancy, le poursuit jusqu'à son terrain à plus de 25 kilometres dans les lignes, mitraillant a bout port les hangars et tuant le pilote. ...Le 10 fevrier, mitraille à faible altitude un terrain d'aviation ennemi. "Le 9 mars, abat un bi-plane ennemi de regulage dans la region de P——, et presqu'immediatement près abat un des monoplace ennemi, d'escorte.*"—Original Editor.

CHAPTER 17

Hits and Misses

After this memorable day there came a lull. Something more than a week passed by, spent in uneventful flying, and my life settled back into the old routine. I continued to fly alone—almost a free lance— the greater part of the time. Within certain limits I was my own dictator, so long as I kept within the scope of duty, which was to guard our front from attack by air, and protect it from hostile observation machines.

On "St. Patrick's day in the morning" I went aloft soon after dawn, and, as the sun climbed up, too, and with his rays swept away the light vapours which departing night had left behind, I decided to vary my uninteresting cruise up and down behind our lines by making a sight-seeing excursion into the enemy's country. My objective was Mittersheim, an aviation field some eighteen miles back of the Hun front lines, and in the vicinity of the spot where Tom had been wounded and captured

Flying after the manner of Geigl at the fairly high altitude of sixty-five hundred metres, from which height the earth begins to lose its details and take on the appearance of a topographical map, not unlike those which you are now seeing in illustrated weeklies, I flew until I had arrived at a point about three and a half miles over the aviation field which was my destination.

Far beneath me it appeared, a diminutive patch of light green bordered by threadlike lines of black,—the trenches—and covered on one side with square pinheads of light gray which I knew were the hangars. Nearer me, by a thousand yards, were three toy machines circling leisurely about, and I was sure that they were German, since the "Archies" on the field had nothing to say to them.

The odds were rather against me, and were increased by the fact that I was far into German territory; but the call of battle was too strong to be withstood that morning. It set my blood a-tingle, and with its chant ringing in my ears I slipped into a moderate *piqué* dive, with my motor still going, and approached them as a cat would three mice at play.

Strangely enough, I managed to get within five hundred yards of them before I, or my true nationality, was discovered. Then their leader sensed something wrong, and signalled to the other two in the usual way.

It was now one of two things for me—fight or flight.

I made up my mind instantly, looked above and about, to make sure that the air was free of other hostile craft, and then went into a vertical dive as straight as an arrow for the last of the trio, who were speeding away as fast as their wings could carry them.

At my superior altitude I had complete mastery of the situation, for the time being at least, and, rushing downward, I gave him my full gunfire fair and square from the point-blank range of fifteen yards.

The pilot toppled, and his plane fell into the spinning nose dive that almost always presages a plummet drop to earth in ruins. Satisfied that I had accounted for him, I made a quick "Russian Mountain" in order to regain my altitude over the other two.

I was successful, turned and dove again, to be mixed up in a "free-for-all" with both of them, a minute later. At my first shot the one on the right slid off into a wing-slip, apparently the recipient of my bullet, and, as the third circled away and headed for home, I followed the other down, firing all the time, and had the glorious satisfaction of seeing his plane smash into a big open field below. My own spiral swoop carried me almost to the ground, and, as I straightened out, barely thirty feet above it, I could plainly see my first victim lying motionless amid the twisted wreckage which had been his machine a few moments before.

The fight and victory had heated my blood to the fever point, and I believe that I actually became delirious for the time being, for, instead of doing the logical thing, and making good my escape from a scrape from which luck had extricated me temporarily, I continued to fly at the dangerously low altitude of a hundred metres. And, as I flew, I shot at every German military thing my eyes fell upon.

The roads were all camouflaged by the erection of strips of painted cheese cloth suspended above them by poles; but they were plainly visible to me from that height, and into auto trucks, artillery and advancing bodies of troops I poured my fire as I sailed above them. I was on the warpath, and again shouting like an Indian.

My mad escapade ended by my turning and sweeping along the first line trench, upon the occupants of which I expended my few remaining cartridges. Not a single one was left when I reached home, unscathed.

The captain was on hand to demand a report of what I had been up to, and, although he repeated the familiar phrase, "*Tous les Américains sont fous*," he smiled delightedly as he said it, and at once telephoned to all the outlying observation posts, to find out if my fight had been officially witnessed.

It had not, of course, having occurred too far into Germany, so I got no credit on the books for my double victory. But I scarcely cared. The fight itself brought satisfaction enough.

That was the beginning of another wave of adventures, and the next one occurred the following morning.

Again there had been coming reports from a district a little to the north of us to the effect that a Boche bi-place machine had been making trips over the French lines to take "*regulage*"—that is, direct the fire of the artillery—and for several days I had been making little jaunts in that direction in the hope of waylaying it, but without success. Its presence had been again signalled on the day when I was paying my call on Mittersheim, but I had been "otherwise engaged." This morning, however, I set out with a definite purpose in view. I was going to "get" the Boche, if he put in an appearance.

The morning was clear, with a moderate wind, and I went up to three thousand metres and slipped leisurely along, well behind the French lines, waiting for the enemy to put in an appearance.

An hour passed without a sign of him, or anything happening to break the monotony of myself appointed patrol; but, just as I was about to start back for the field, I saw him coming. His plane was flying swiftly into France at not more than eight hundred metres from the ground.

To my astonishment he came directly on toward a point almost beneath me. Either he had not caught sight of me at all, or was relying upon his own excellent camouflage to conceal him from my sight. Indeed, it might have, if I had not been on the keen lookout for him, so remarkably did his machine blend with the earth below.

When he had obligingly entered the trap which I had laid for him, I *piquéd* and then started a vertical dive directly behind him. At the same instant the pilot saw me coming, made a quick vertical *virage* and headed for home. My falcon swoop brought me below him, just over No-Man's-Land and, doing a "Russian Mountain" and *renversement*, I fired several shots, and then went into a side wing-slip to save myself from continuing upward and passing close to him, which would have given his gunner a clean shot at me. Would have—that is—if he had been alive to take advantage of it; but, as I sped away, and upward to regain my altitude, I saw that my gunfire had ended his fighting days forever.

Repeating the same procedure I attacked again and again without scoring a decisive hit, and by the time I was ready to start my fifth dive we were both well into German territory, although I scarcely realized it in my deep absorption.

Just as I pushed my control stick forward to lower my rear *ailerons* and shoot downward, I heard the spiteful banging of a *mitrailleuse*, and simultaneously a tell-tale streak of light passed from the rear almost between the planes of my machine. It was a "tracer" bullet, of course, and brought a pointed warning that more company had arrived.

My head flew around and I saw a pair of *Albatros* machines above and behind me, all set for an attack. Now I dove with a double purpose. I planned instantly to use my original enemy as a shield, if possible, and, with this in view, I manoeuvred to get fairly close beneath him. Then, by watching the movement of his rudder and rear *ailerons*, and duplicating it exactly, I followed his every turn, and, being the more speedy, kept creeping closer and closer all the time.

I had him in a corner, and was taking no chances by firing before I was certain of making my shot tell.

Then, just as my finger was curving about the trigger, one of the *Albatros* planes dove past me, brushing by so close that I might almost have reached out and touched him. He failed to distract my attention, however; my *mitrailleuse* spoke and called the pilot into eternity. The big machine turned sharply, like an animal which has received its death wound, and, out of control, went spinning down to destruction.

Quite content to let well enough alone this time, I started a spiral climb by means of which I quickly outdistanced the other two, although one of them made a futile attack before I got wholly free.

This was my third unofficial victory in two days, for it, too, had occurred too far behind the Hun lines to have been observed and recorded in my favour.

The final fight of my brief flying career at that time took place about a week later. I was patrolling alone as usual, and was over No-Man's-Land when I came upon a monoplane Boche plane doing the same stunt.

His machine was an *Albatros*, and in speed and gunfire almost exactly equal to mine. He also turned out to be my equal, either in efficiency or inefficiency, as the case may have been, and for fully twenty minutes we manoeuvred about one another, doing all the tricks known to aviation and apparently having chances innumerable to dispatch one another. Every one of them went to waste, and at last I fired my final cartridge and turned toward home, fully expecting him to pursue and make the most of his opportunity.

Instead, he, too, turned homeward, and I concluded that he, like myself, had exhausted his ammunition. And as we parted we waved each other farewell.

Probably he was hoping, as I was, that we might meet another time and try our rivalry out to a conclusion.

Chapter 18

Two Miracles

It is not every man who can say that, in one day, he was the victim of one miracle, and had his life saved by another. I can, truthfully; but the combination put a sudden end to my flying—temporarily, at least.

This happened on the twenty-first day of March, just about four months after I had started my real work. The day dawned gloriously, giving no premonition that it had anything out of the ordinary in store for me, and I completed an uneventful morning patrol and was up in the air again about four in the afternoon. Over the American trenches and No-Man's-Land I flew with no particular object in view, other than to keep a sharp lookout for Boche machines. None were in sight, which was not at all unusual, for at this time we had a fair control of the air in our sector and they seldom bothered us, unless there was some special reason for so doing.

In fact everything was quiet, above and below, and the earth seemed wrapped in Springtime somnambulance. Back and forth I flew at an altitude of fifty-three hundred metres, guiding my plane by instinct as you might a bicycle, and thinking of almost everything but war, and personal danger. There was no enemy in the air to attract my attention, and I had long since ceased to worry about the "Archies." These anti-aircraft guns were a standing joke with us, as I have said. As a method of keeping airplanes at a respectable distance from earth by means of a barrage of bursting shrapnel they are of some value; but an actual hit by them is nothing short of a miracle, which is hardly strange when one considers the diminutive size and the tremendous speed of the airy target at which they have to fire.

Then, with the utmost unexpectedness, occurred the first miracle. Out of the clear sky came a blinding flash in my; face; a crashing detonation in my ears. Half-stunned for a second, I closed my eyes, then opened them to a realization that my plane was pointing perpendicularly downward and spinning rapidly. A solitary shell from a Boche "Archie" had exploded directly in front of me and into the hole which it had torn in the air my machine had dived automatically.

It took me a perceptible amount of time to get my mind sufficiently cleared of the daze which the explosion had brought, so that I could rightly understand what had happened. Then I concluded that I was neither dead nor injured, and—thanking my lucky star for another narrow escape—I cut off my motor and drew back my control stick to bring my plane out of its plunging descent.

Nothing happened. With a feeling merely of utter surprise, I tried again. Still I continued to rush earthward, head first and whirling. The awful truth began to dawn upon me. I looked around and upward at the tail of my *fuselage*. Part of the canvas there was flapping violently, and now the full terrifying fact rushed over my mind. *The flying shrapnel had scored a clean hit.* My back control wires were shot away, my rear *ailerons* were out of commission, and I was completely helpless. Below me, still nearly three miles distant, but rising with appalling speed, was the hard earth. I needed no one to tell me what was going to happen in a few seconds when we two met.

There may be men who can face the prospect of certain and immediate death with cool courage and unconcern; if so, I am not of their number. I was so frightened that for an instant all my physical powers became as weak as water, and I discovered the truth of the saying that the events of a drowning man's past life flash before his mind. Certainly I thought of a whole lot of sins of omission and commission that my past held; I thought of my little mother at home, and I prayed, not as the scribes do, but with my whole heart.

Then a friendly current of air—sent, perhaps, in answer to that prayer, who knows?—changed my spinning nose dive into a sweeping spiral, for my side controls were all right; but, from a height of twenty-five hundred metres, I continued to speed downward, helpless, and although a little slower than before, no less inexorably.

I was in the clutch of circumstances over which no mortal could possibly have any control, and the utter helplessness of my position now brought a mental reaction. My prayers turned to profanity, and I raged impotently against the Fate toward which I was rushing.

The drift of the light wind was, I saw, carrying me northwestward, and by the time my machine had almost reached the ground it was over the forest of Parroy.

Close above a forest there is almost always a layer of dead air. So it was that day, and when my plane reached it and I felt that my last second had come, its nose shot upward and the spiral turned into a side wing-slip. Instantly there came to me the thought that I might yet have a chance for life, and I banged my fist against the fastening of my belt. It sprang open, liberating me, and at the same instant I felt my machine strike with terrific force among the tree tops.

Whether I voluntarily jumped free of it, or was thrown out by the shock, I cannot say; but, as the most of it went on earthward with a sound of tearing canvas and snapping wood, to crash, rent and shattered, on the ground beneath, I remained clinging to one of the topmost boughs of a big fir tree.

For a second I was again too dazed to realize the truth—then came the knowledge that I was still alive, saved from a death which had seemed inevitable, by a second miracle.

Now there came a torturing pain in my back, which had been struck and badly wrenched, and a feeling of complete weakness and nausea.

I could scarcely move, but I could not stay where I was, in a most unpleasant and still precarious position, and, with much difficulty, and very slowly, I half slid, half scrambled down the life-saving tree.

Every movement brought a new stab of pain, my back felt so weak that I thought it was broken, and I had to clinch my teeth and make a determined mental effort in order to keep going; but I reached the ground at last, and sank down beside the wreck of the "CELIA V," for a time too overcome by pain and weakness even to be thankful.

At a distance I heard the sound of running feet and excited voices calling to me, but I could not answer them. Something seemed to be stinging near my eye. I mechanically put my hand to the place, and brought it away covered with blood.

Then, for the first time, I realized that I had been injured other than in my back, and I found out later that a piece of the shrapnel had struck and imbedded itself in my nose, not more than an eighth of an inch from the eyeball.

When the five or six *poilus*, who had witnessed my fall, arrived on the scene, they found me on my hands and knees, too weak to speak. I felt them pick me up and lay me on my back, then a black wave swept over me and I lost consciousness.

When I came to, it was to look up into the faces of a French army doctor and two French nurses. One was bathing my head and stroking it gently. I shall never see a nurse's uniform without blessing it. They tried to keep me down, but I insisted upon sitting up immediately, and did it, too, although I felt mighty dizzy.

"Your back received a pretty bad wrench and blow," said the physician, kindly. "How do you feel?"

"I feel fine," I answered, with the assistance of the nurses struggling to my feet. And although they wanted to summon an ambulance to take me home, I refused.

The doctor aided me to a dugout under a ruined stone farmhouse near the third line trenches, from which I telephoned to our field for a motor car to come and get me. It arrived at length, and, as I still insisted that I was all right, and really felt fairly well, he let me go alone. I was driven up to the *Pilotage*, walked in and saluted Captain Azire, saying, "*Mon Capitaine*, I have to report that I have just been shot down by an anti-aircraft gun from fifty-three hundred metres over the forest of Parroy."

He looked at me in amazement, and answered, "*Mon Dieu*. Are you badly hurt? Do you want me to send for our doctor?"

"No, my captain, I'm all right, but my beautiful plane is a complete wreck." I told him where he could locate it, and he said that if I were sure I did not need attention, he would motor out at once and look it over.

Leaving him, I went at once to my room in the *château*, which I now had all to myself, called my orderly and, with his aid, undressed and got into bed. Now I was beginning to feel very weak again, and rather strange inside. The orderly rubbed my back with alcohol, and from five o'clock—the hour at which I turned in—until daylight the next morning I tried to sleep, but the pain in my back increased steadily until my suffering was severe. Then the orderly put in his appearance, brought me bread and butter and chocolate, and I got him to give my back another rub.

Captain Azire came to see me early that morning, and, finding me unable to get up, and considerably worse than I had allowed him to suspect, or had, indeed, suspected myself, he sent for the doctor connected with our corps.

The latter came, gave me a thorough examination, a rub and a sleeping powder and told me to remain in bed until I felt strong enough to travel. "Then," he said, "you must go and see Dr. Tuffier, the famous Parisian surgeon." During that day, and each which followed, my comrades came in to visit me whenever they were off duty, and told me all about what was happening, but they carefully refrained from discussing my accident, other than to congratulate me upon my luck in being alive.

It was three days before I had strength and ambition enough to get up and make the journey to Paris, and by the time I reached the city I felt so weak and rocky again that it was about all that I could do to crawl from the train to a taxicab and direct the driver to take me to the doctor's hospital.

The name "Tuffier" is well known in France, for the surgeon is one of the world's leading authorities on lung wounds. I was ushered at once into the office of that distinguished-looking, elderly marvel, and had the honour, after he had made an examination of me, of being taken by him through part of the hospital, in one room of which he showed me a famous "case," a *poilu* who had been shot through the lung, and whose right breast was all laid open and filled with tubes for breathing and drainage. When I looked on that horribly shattered man, who, the doctor said, would live, although a few years before he would have been doomed with such a wound, I felt almost ashamed of my own minor injuries.

However, Dr. Tuffier had said, after finishing looking me over, that my back had received a bad bruise and strain and that the blow had also affected me internally.

He also said that I should most certainly be "*reformé*" (discharged from the army) and return home to rest and recuperate. If I did this I would recover in a few months.

Although I had been looking forward to a possible leave, the idea of going at that time had not entered my head; but, when I heard his words my heart jumped joyfully, and I instantly knew that there was nothing else on earth that I wanted to do so much as get back to America in a hurry. Killing Boches could not compare with it as an impelling desire, for, although my fall had not cured me of my eagerness to fly and fight, my ambition along those lines had waned with the coming of my great physical weakness.

"Go back to Lunéville," he commanded, "and wait for your orders. I will write to your division commander a personal recommendation for your discharge."

I obeyed his instructions, and for three days more remained quiet, resting, eating and sleeping. Then the mail brought me a brief order from the chief of the Eighth Army at Nancy, which instructed me to appear at headquarters there at ten a. m. on March the twenty-ninth.

When I reached the office at the place and time appointed I found the colonel commanding our Southwestern division, a major or two, and several captains assembled in conclave. The first-mentioned greeted me pleasantly, and, while I stood at attention, he read a brief summary of my career in the French army, enlistment and record of my victories and of having been shot down and wounded. Then he said, "The Board has recommended that you receive the *reformé*. Number two—which means an honourable discharge."

I saluted, thanked him and stepped out into the Spring sunshine as happy as ever I had been in my life. *I was going home.*

My return to Lunéville, packing up, final farewells, and the journey to Paris were all accomplished in record time. Once there, my first act was to call upon Mr. Thaw of the United States Consulate, and make application for my passport.

It was three weeks before this would be ready for me, and I spent the time very quietly.

In one respect I found Paris considerably changed. You have read that the populace laugh at *Big Bertha*, the Huns' devilling gun that sends its shells into the city from seventy-five miles away. It is not true; at least it was not true in April. They were not terror-stricken by any means, nor was their *morale* badly shaken by that new, uncanny menace—which is in reality much less dangerous than the air raiders to whom they have become accustomed—but it had certainly gotten on their nerves. As airplanes could generally be detected in advance, the *Alerte* gave noisy warning of their approach, and the people might, if they wished, dive for cellars and subways. But *Big Bertha's* evil offspring came without warning, other than its own whistle, which was not a warning but a signal that it had passed.

Even the sound that *it* makes is very slight, nor nearly as loud as the drowning hum or shriek of the big gun's shells at the front, and it is, therefore, a horrible, silent peril which cannot be guarded against in any fashion, and takes its hellish toll as indiscriminately as Fate herself.

Many of the richer people left Paris hastily after it began its work, the people of the hotel told me.

The newspapers generally made only the briefest mention of its toll of innocent lives; but on Good Friday the wrath of the whole city burst into flames over the detailed report that scores of worshipers had been slaughtered while kneeling in church, and, as I read of this

CERTIFICATE OF MEMBERSHIP IN THE LAFAYETTE FLYING CORPS
AWARDED TO MR. WELLMAN

crime, and heard it discussed everywhere by people whose lips were drawn back and hands clinched with hate and horror, my one hot anger against the Hun was rekindled. I was going home and I was glad; but I swore that I would return soon, if Fate were willing, and take up my small part of the work of crushing the evil. On Easter Sunday the weapon of frightfulness claimed many more innocent victims, this time in a maternity hospital. It was a glorious day for Germany. She had snuffed out a score more prospective French soldiers, in being or yet to be!

One day, a little later, I was walking by the side of the River Seine. Its surface was covered with dead fish. A shell from *Big Bertha* had struck and exploded in it that morning, a *gendarme* told me.

This sort of thing, violent death striking down wholesale everything which lives, is the daily lot of Paris. When it comes to New York, Boston or other big cities, perhaps Americans will learn how to hate the Hun as he deserves.

During my period of waiting for the passport I had another slight operation, the piece of shrapnel being taken from the wound near my eye. Otherwise my stay was uneventful as far as personal experiences went, and the receipt of my permission to return to America, the trip to Bordeaux, and the voyage home on the *Espagne* were all undistinguished by anything of peculiar interest. They are not part of my story of that eventful twelve months, and have no place in it.

If such a narration can have a moral, this is it, and it is drawn from my own personal experiences.

We cannot afford to take the Hun lightly, or take anything for granted in connection with Germany. He is a terrible fighter; she is a terrible world-menace. Every now and then we read in the daily papers that a number of Boche soldiers have surrendered, starved, worn out and glad to be prisoners. Doubtless all this is true, but it is highly unsafe to draw any general conclusions from such reports. The German soldier may be driven to fight, but he *can* fight, and will.

There is no use in blinding ourselves to the obvious fact that, if the war should stop now, Germany would be the winner. We have got to *beat* the Boche, whether it takes one year or ten, and, as the Captain of the Blue Devils who have lately been touring America put it, "We don't know how long the war is going to last, but it will last until someone is beaten—and it will not be we!"

In telling my story to many audiences since I returned home I have never lost an opportunity to say that we airmen are not the heroes that we are acclaimed. I say it now. Flying is safe, under ordinary conditions, and under extraordinary ones it is nine-tenths luck—and the other tenth is foolishness. It is the men in the trenches who are the real heroes of this war, for theirs is the hardest work; theirs the most horrible conditions.

All honour to them, yet I cannot but believe that the war will be won in the air, and only when the Allies have established a *complete* supremacy there. Every military man knows that the aircraft are the eyes of a modern army, and, if we can wholly blind the Prussian eagle, the battle will be half won.

Besides, they have of late become a new factor in land fighting, and a large squadron of them, equipped with rapid-fire guns, and flying low over moving masses of the enemy's troops, can rake them at short range and accomplish, with comparatively little danger, more than a hundred or a thousand times their number on foot. The war has assumed a new phase, one of movement, and the "cavalry of the air" will play the most important part in it, I firmly believe.

The French bore the burden of air fighting at first, and bore it nobly; England, with her wonderful "Royal Flying Corps," is now assuming the Lion's share, and America has begun to do her part. It is highly fitting that, before the war is ended, we should assume the *Eagle's* share of this all-important work.

American youths are, by racial characteristics and training, particularly well fitted to take the lead in this greatest of all games, and, since America gave being to the first airplane, she should now resume supremacy in its use—a supremacy which she should never have lost.

We need, not hundreds, nor thousands, but tens of thousands of airplanes, trained aviators and mechanics at the front, and need them there immediately.

Wake up, America, and stretch your wings, the wings of Victory!